DATE DUE

SEP 2 4 2011

THE TRANSPARENT LEADER

THE TRANS

HOW TO BUILD A GREAT COMPANY THROUG

HARPERBUSINESS

AN IMPRINT OF HARPERCOLLINS*PUBLISHERS*

PARENT LEADER

TRAIGHT TALK, OPENNESS, AND ACCOUNTABILITY

HERB BAUM

with Tammy Kling

HarperCollins books may be purchased for educational, business,
or sales promotional use. For information please write: Special
Markets Department, HarperCollins Publishers Inc., 10 East 53rd
Street, New York, NY 10022.

FIRST EDITION

Designed by Ellen Cipriano

Library of Congress Cataloging-in-Publication Data has been
applied for.

ISBN 0-06-056547-0

04 05 06 07 08 DIX/QW 10 9 8 7 6 5 4 3 2 1

To all those who go through life as "goody two-shoes."
God bless you.

"Surround yourself with the best people you can find, delegate authority, and don't interfere."

—RONALD REAGAN

CONTENTS

ACKNOWLEDGMENTS

Many thanks to all the employees, colleagues, and friends who helped me during my career running four different consumer products companies. I've been involved in food products, motor oil, toys, and household products, and I've enjoyed every bit of it and especially the great people I met along the way. I owe a great debt of gratitude to them for what they taught me about going through life, and everything I have done came from those relationships.

Special thanks to my friend and business associate Steve Blum, whom I've known more than twenty years. Steve has seen my management style in action more than anyone and has played an important part in shaping the way I do business. He was a tireless supporter of this book and was absolutely certain that my leadership philosophy of openness, integrity, and a no-holds-barred approach to communications would be of interest to other executives and business leaders. I hope readers will find this to be the case.

Thank you to Tammy Kling, my co-author, a former executive in corporate America and the author of several books, who, along with Steve and me, came up with the concept for a book that would help others lead transparently. Tammy made this book a reality during one of the busiest years of my life, and I am grateful for her intelligence and her listening and translation skills.

Thanks to Knox Huston, Dave Conti, and all of the competent and insightful people at HarperCollins for developing this book into what it is.

Finally, the most important thanks of all go to my wife and best friend, Karen, who has always had a higher opinion of my executive leadership skills than I have. Though my tendency is to maintain a low profile, I am sincerely grateful to her for driving me to do this book. Karen has believed in me as a goody two-shoes and knows that I'm *her* goody two-shoes.

FOREWORD

When I first reflected on what it means to be a transparent leader, I'll admit, I didn't think of nearly all the angles Herb covers in this book. I agreed to share my thoughts on transparency while envisioning a few paragraphs on the Internet and how that channel has moved us at lightning speed from an era of "hiding in the Ivory Tower" to one of open access, chat rooms, and message boards. In this new environment, ideas and opinions are shared, no holds barred, and there's nowhere to hide!

But while the Internet may have eased transparency, it did not create it, nor is it the sole driver behind living as a transparent leader. Herb offers the three principles every successful transparent organization should practice. Summed up in five short words, Herb inspires us to *tell it like it is.* And nowhere was this mantra more necessary than in the airline industry during the aftermath of 9/11.

On September 10, 2001, out of all of the airlines operating in the United States, America West had the least amount of cash for its operating size. With a government-imposed cessation of flying for four days following 9/11, and the understandable concern among passengers about the safety and security of air travel, this meant America West had the shortest amount of time to live. Those words are difficult to write even today, but imagine having to say them in front of 13,000 employees, numerous state and local government officials, and our nation's Congress. Perhaps most painful was admitting to the nearly 20 million people who travel with America West each year that we might not be there for them in the future.

I had only been CEO for ten days on September 11, 2001, and certainly hadn't planned on being in this situation. But faced with it, we relied on the values that had worked in the past. We came clean—describing our situation with brutal candor to all who would listen. Once we did, an amazing thing happened. People we'd never dreamed of asking for help started calling to offer assistance. (Not surprisingly, Herb Baum was one of those people, which is how Herb and I met . . . thanks again, Herb.) Our employees pulled together, the communities we served rallied to support us, and our key suppliers came through with critical financial assistance. In the end, we secured the funds needed to keep our airplanes flying and our people employed, while ensuring our customers retained their option to conduct business in person or to visit family and friends.

No matter how painful, telling the truth was the right thing to do then. It remains our philosophy today and guides every decision at America West, and I am convinced that operating under this core value has been a key driver in our successful turnaround.

But telling it like it is is not just a call for action during times of crisis. At America West, taking a hard look at everything we had become, admitting where we had made mistakes, and taking courageous steps to undo those mistakes and reinvent ourselves have provided the second chapter in our successful turnaround. Herb reminds us that these are sometimes the most difficult decisions organizations must make. Knowing when to undo and start over only occurs after we've first admitted the truth to ourselves.

For any service business, but especially for an airline, your business is only as good as the values under which your people operate. Building a culture based on values takes time, truth, and transparency. Herb's experiences provide counsel and inspiration to business leaders at any level. He reminds us that it is never too early or too late to begin living as a transparent leader.

—Doug Parker, CEO,
America West Airlines

INTRODUCTION

About two years ago I decided to write a book. The corporate world was reeling from scandal, on the heels of major indictments and investigations at big companies such as MCI WorldCom, Rite Aid, Enron, and others. As I sat and watched the television reports of major executives handcuffed and led away by investigators, I was puzzled. I've had a long career in corporate America, and it seems to me that it would be hard to get yourself in that position. I've always believed in doing the right thing in business and in life, and it hasn't been easy! I'm by no means perfect, but I do know one thing—honesty and transparency is the only way. But there is a fundamental problem in corporate America today, and it's a lack of *transparency.*

Throughout the year following all that corporate scandal, I knew that this book would have to address the transparency problem and offer solutions for the leaders of tomorrow. I wanted to let executives of all ages know that cutting corners, lying, and taking shortcuts aren't good strategies to get you to the top. There are a few critical building blocks necessary to become a transparent leader, and in this book you'll learn about all of them and how to apply them to your business—regardless of the business you're in. If you don't learn now, you'll be forced to sooner or later, because transparency isn't just the latest corporate buzzword. It's a long-term lifestyle commitment, and every industry's consumers, shareholders, and activist groups are looking for it. Transparency is the new asset.

I've been practicing transparent leadership for my entire career. I know that it's impossible to be a great leader, or even a good one, if you're not transparent. You may achieve a lot of goals, and you might even appear on the cover of a national business magazine, but if you're not transparent your successes won't last very long. Transparency simply means being honest and open in everything you do. It means making values-based decisions and fessing up when you make a mistake. It's a management style that has served me well over the years, and it will do the same for you.

Transparency is the only true way to run your company, but unfortunately, there are a lot of executives who still don't understand this. A lot of the things in the corporate world have changed as a result of leaders who acted without transparency, and without much in the way of a commitment to corporate and personal ethics. As my friend and fellow board member Bob Pohlad, the CEO of PepsiAmericas says: "Where were their mothers?"

But in the corporate world, for a lot of executives, doing the right thing is not quite so easy as it once was—mainly because society and what it deems acceptable has become far more relaxed. There no longer seems to be a firm consensus on what constitutes what is right as opposed to what is wrong, and as a result we all tend to forgive or forget with equal ease. And when we're no longer focusing on the fundamental issue of doing business *transparently,* the building blocks of the business break down. Things like honesty and integrity. Things like service.

My inspiration in writing this book was the lack of service in corporate America—something that stems from a lack of values, and a "who cares?" attitude. Providing good service is just one byproduct of being a transparent leader, because offering customers exceptional service and developing employees who care about their customers and colleagues comes from the top. It stems from a leader's genuine desire to be open, honest, and transparent, and it has a trickle-down effect. If a leader is open to customers' suggestions and employee feedback, the result is good service. If a leader is honest about the company's mistakes, customers will notice. Good or bad service is the direct result of how *transparent* a company is—which is a direct result of the way the CEO thinks and acts.

A common thread behind the success of the companies I have been involved with over the years has been each organization's ability to anticipate and recognize what consumers want and deliver it with outstanding service. But you can't provide good service without being transparent—because sooner or later your lack of genuine concern will be discovered, and whatever you were not being open and honest about will be revealed. That's not good service, it's deception, and a lot of business leaders have found out the hard way that it doesn't work.

This book is about being a transparent leader and why it's important to do business with integrity. It's about my personal view that doing the right thing means doing it regardless of circumstances and regardless of consequences. Nevertheless, I hope readers will pick up on the message that doing the right thing (being transparent) has a ton of upside, including what I believe is a great way to go through life.

As a matter of fact, I began my commitment to honesty early in my life. When I was growing up, my sister always referred to me as "goody two-shoes," a taunting phrase that signaled my penchant for never breaking the rules and trying always to do the right thing. My wife, Karen, has picked up on the goody two-shoes phrase. I guess I've been consistent, and it's a nickname I won't be able to shake.

Finally, there will be downsides to transparency. People and organizations will try to take advantage of you when they know your business and life strategy. Bad things *do* happen to good people, but this downside is not insurmountable. As Grantland Rice answered it best, "It's not whether you win or lose. It's how you play the game." Be transparent, and your life and business will reap great rewards.

PART ONE
THE POWER OF TRANSPARENCY

When most executives think about the best way to increase revenues, manage employees, or gain market share from their competitors they think of a strategy or a program, not a core value. A value is something we learn from our parents—a guideline or belief that helps us through life, not in business dealings. Values such as integrity and honesty aren't competitive tools. Or are they?

In today's business environment, if you're a leader—or want to be—and you aren't contributing to a values-based business culture that encourages your entire organization to operate with integrity, your company is as vulnerable as a baby chick in a pit of rattlesnakes. Transparency—the art of being completely open and honest in business—is a competitive tool. It's something that must be learned, honed, and perfected. How important is it? We've all read about whole companies that have been toppled because their leaders didn't know how to incorporate values into their business processes. Not only did they have a "what's in it for me?" attitude, but they brought employees, their families, and their futures to financial ruin.

Through the three chapters in Part One—"The Transparent Company," "The Transparent Leader," and "The Transparent Employee"—you'll learn about the power of transparency, and why it's critical in today's business environment. You'll gain an understanding of how service-oriented employees contribute to a transparent organization, the rewards of telling it like it is, and how to define your business culture to cultivate an ethical workplace.

CHAPTER ONE

THE TRANSPARENT COMPANY

The air in the conference room was somber. As a member of the board, I had been asked to cast my vote for the forced resignation of the reigning CEO.

The board meeting was held at the Broadmoor Hotel in Colorado Springs, a resort nestled in the shadows of the Rocky Mountains. Earlier in the day I met the CEO for a casual lunch in the hotel restaurant, along with the company's senior vice president of human resources. It was a great day. Or so I thought.

We had a casual lunch at an outdoor table, and the conversation was upbeat. The Dial Corporation's CEO, Malcolm Jozoff, acknowledged that earnings were slipping, but he was certain that things would soon turn around. None of us at the table sensed what lay ahead, and even Malcolm was completely unaware of the perilous events about to unfold in his career.

Jozoff was a vigorous man with stark white hair. He was an avid runner, and sometimes could be seen running in the neighborhood around Dial headquarters in Scottsdale, Arizona, at lunchtime. A graduate of Columbia University, he had arrived at Dial after two years as the chairman and chief executive officer of Lenox, Inc., a division of Brown-Forman that sold china and crystal.

Mal had had a long career with Procter & Gamble that gave him a good background for managing a company like Dial. As a CEO he was confident (perhaps arrogant at times) and, as it turned out, not totally communicative with the board about the businesses' problems. As a member of that very board, I began to feel that Dial—the company he had led for five years—was headed for trouble. Dial had missed earnings estimates for three consecutive quarters. The employees described the atmosphere along executive row as oppressive, employee turnover was high, and Jozoff seemed to have no solid succession plan in place, a necessity for any good leader. At prior board meetings I had listened carefully while Jozoff and his executive team outlined strategies for growing the business, and on the day we lunched together at the Broadmoor, I had no indication that it would be his last meeting as CEO, an unceremonious end to a long and stellar business career.

When the members of the board convened in the hotel meeting room we took our seats, approved the minutes, and immediately elected a new director! It was Jim Osterreicher, the retired chairman and CEO of the J.C. Penney Company, Inc. Then, as we got into the meeting, one board member spoke up and asked that we break into executive session—a meeting that would exclude everyone on the corporate management team, *including* the CEO. For seconds there was silence. Malcolm seemed surprised, but then again so were the rest of us. Someone cleared his throat. The room was quiet, and Malcolm stood and quickly left.

The board member who called the session was the retired CEO of a major telecommunications company. He explained that some senior Dial executives had come to him with legitimate concerns about the health of the business and the tactics being used to build sales. We listened to what he had to say, digested the information, and thought about solutions.

There were nine people on the Dial board, among them the CEO of a major telecommunications provider, the CEO of a paper corporation, and two very talented women, one who at the time was the president and chief operating officer of an Abbott Labs subsidiary. I had been on a lot of boards, but this one was by far the most governance-oriented and aggressive panel of executives I'd worked with, and they represented a variety of industries.

The board discussed the employee allegations. We had to take into account that these were just allegations, not documented facts, but we all knew that earnings had declined significantly, sales had slowed, and that the stock price was in a free fall.

After we evaluated the information presented, we all came to the same conclusion: it was time for a change. We decided that the CEO hadn't been completely open and honest but instead had painted a rosy picture even when things weren't so good. He hadn't been completely forthright about the company's problems, and we felt we had no choice but to vote for his resignation.

No one enjoys casting a vote to end someone's career or turn it in a different direction. That's the tough part of being a board member. But the Dial board acted quickly and responsibly by opting for a no-nonsense approach designed to purge the company's problems and breathe life into it again. There wasn't any scandal to speak of, but things sure weren't getting any better, and in the absence of total disclosure we wondered what other skeletons might be lurking in the management team's closet.

THE OPAQUE COMPANY

A lot of business leaders found themselves in the same position in recent years. In the time period between 1995 and 2001 alone, CEO turnover at major corporations had increased 53 percent. Fifty-three percent!

It seems a day hasn't gone by without a major headline concerning a scandal involving a company CEO, which is a sad sign of the times when you consider that at some point in their careers they had been considered highly qualified. After all, they had to be to get the job in the first place! They had a lot of the traits found in other leaders, like intelligence, charisma, creativity, and vision. So if they had all that going for them, why did they fail?

The answer isn't simple. A lot of the executives who made headlines were just plain white-collar thieves who deserved to do time. And there were others who were basically good people who made compromises when they shouldn't have. They stretched the truth because they thought they had to, and they made some business decisions that were short on integrity. They had risen to leadership positions, but they failed because they didn't understand how to be open with their various constituents and they were unable to build a culture based on trust in the organizations they led.

THE TRANSPARENT COMPANY

Transparency is the single largest challenge facing corporate America today, and it will continue to be as long as CEOs and other executives fail to subscribe to a values-based approach to leadership. Let me elaborate on that a bit. You might *become* successful without being open, honest, and transparent, but if you don't adopt a transparent management style, your success will be short-lived. It'll disappear as fast as it came, or one day you'll wake up to find that you're being investigated because you didn't do things the right way.

Transparency is a critical business practice. It's not a strategy, and it's not something a trendy consultant can teach. Executives have a business and social responsibility to tell it like it is. You can't build a transparent company without it.

Let's take a look at what a transparent company looks like.

A transparent company can be defined as one that's rooted in core values, based on the greatest good for the greatest number of people, with a leader who believes in doing the right thing at all times—no matter what the consequences. That means following the rules, no matter how boring that may sound, and telling it like it is, as hard as that may seem. The transparent company fosters a *culture* of openness and inclusion, and therefore is able to adapt to unexpected shifts in market conditions by simply doing the right thing.

There are three principles a transparent company *must* have:

- a leader who believes in telling the whole truth
- a values-based corporate culture
- employees who are "people people" (service-oriented/team players)

PRINCIPLE NUMBER 1: TELL THE WHOLE TRUTH

The first principle defies conventional thinking about business strategy and what it takes to succeed. You have to tell the truth at all times. Some might say that to tell the whole truth is to show your cards, to let down your guard, to give up leverage in negotiations. Is it? The answer will surprise you.

At Dial it wasn't one flagrant violation that caused the former CEO's downfall, it was a series of missteps, and when sales and earnings continued to deteriorate, the management team compounded the errors until it was too late to stop the avalanche.

In late 1999 and early 2000, the company fell short of expected results quarter after quarter, and the management team began to lose credibility with shareholders. There were ill-fated acquisitions going back to 1999, such as the purchase of a second-rate Argentinean detergent-and-soap business that involved brands that were too local and had no synergies with the strong brands Dial marketed in the U.S. Management had concluded there was only limited growth to be had in the U.S. market, so they went to Argentina. But when the Argentinean market heated up, Dial found its small local Argentinean brands entrenched in a price war between soap giants Unilever and Procter & Gamble. It was a classic mistake. By expanding internationally with local brands, Dial drifted into unchartered territory, where it lacked the strong brand leverage it had in the U.S. market. But that's not the end of the story.

Dial's CEO also pushed for the purchase of Freeman Cosmetics and Sara Michaels, two specialty personal-care businesses in which Dial had little expertise, no legitimate infrastructure, and no real plan to compete successfully. Dial's internal acquisition review team advised against it, but senior management ignored them and moved forward anyway.

Overall, Dial's corporate business strategy seemed unfocused, and growth objectives were lofty. There were too many sales promotions scheduled at the end of each quarter that did little more than boost company sales and customer inventories, and nothing for *customer* sell-through or *consumer* consumption. This was all done in an effort to meet unrealistic sales goals. It was a dangerous practice, because common sense tells you that if you ship more product than can be consumed, all you do is fill up customer warehouses, and eventually your sales—even at discounted prices—will back up on you. Dial's management had shown sales increases for several quarters, but when customers' inventories began to build up, sales slowed to a crawl. This is where Jozoff failed. He didn't face up to the mistakes. He just kept going, doing the same thing, and he violated the first principle of transparency. Show your cards. Admit when you have a problem. Then fix it.

By the time I arrived, I learned that there had been a lot of compromises at Dial in the past that violated the basic principles of transparency I believed in. The corporate culture was repressed, Dial's cash was dwindling, its debt was growing, and management hadn't subscribed to the principle of telling it like it is—the whole truth, warts and all. The employees and the board of directors had been kept in the dark and the company was in trouble.

Dial's management didn't understand that an *open culture*—where the CEO, the management team, and all employees tell the truth—is a competitive tool. Dial had a lot of talented people, but what had been considered acceptable business practice wasn't acceptable to me as the new CEO. I've been a part of successful turnarounds before, and when you realize how different the culture of the company is from what you know it has to be, you know you've got to take bold steps to turn things around. It's an evolving process, and it can't happen quickly, because first you have to earn credibility in the eyes of a skeptical employee population.

We had to work hard to reverse the type of mind-set that led to those compromises and business practices in the first place, so the first step we took was to address the most obvious problem, which was the lack of clear and transparent reporting of product sales. Initially, we moved to compare actual sales with consumer consumption. Sounds simple, but that's not what had been happening. By tracking actual sales against the rate of consumption, we took a step in the direction toward a more truthful business picture, because we didn't oversell to fill customers' warehouses, building unrealistic customer inventories. Principle number 1: *Tell the whole truth.*

We began telling the whole truth by reporting a cross section of average quarterly customer warehouse inventories of our key products each quarter to the Dial board of directors and the investment community, until inventories were normalized. We had to turn things around as fast as possible to get the company back on track, and we overcommunicated with everyone involved. Credibility was our primary goal.

We gave detailed updates to stock-market analysts, granted interviews with media when asked, and laid out our plans for a turnaround. Once we did that, we were committed. Now came the hard part: we had to produce results! You have to be crystal clear about your intentions when it comes to change, because even the most comprehensive turnaround plan will fail without total disclosure.

I let our employees know that there would be zero tolerance for selling product to customers for any other purpose than consumption, and that anyone who sold to load our customers' warehouses would be fired. No forgiveness. No second chances. Sound harsh? Maybe, but we had to establish a new business protocol that would reflect the highest standards. We needed to change not only attitudes, but behavior.

Why Not Hide the Truth Until Things Get Better?

Three years after the Dial CEO was voted out, it felt like déjà vu as I cast my vote to oust the CEO of the Fleming Companies, a giant food wholesaler. Mark Hansen, Fleming's CEO, had forgotten the first principle of transparency and had kept his board, his shareowners, and the Fleming employees isolated from the real facts about the company's poor performance and data that showed the company was in trouble. He made several critical errors, including downplaying the loss of the Kmart wholesale distribution. Kmart was a major Fleming customer, one that accounted for 15 to 20 percent of Fleming's revenue. The Kmart business had been worth an estimated $4.5 billion in annual sales for the company, but when Kmart filed for bankruptcy, Hansen downplayed the impact it would have on Fleming. Illegal? Not at all. Unethical? Probably not. But Hansen violated a fundamental aspect of being a transparent leader—total honesty and openness. After the Kmart bankruptcy, Fleming was left with more employees, inventory, and warehouses than it could support with its remaining business. Had he not seen it coming? In hindsight, it's hard to imagine that he didn't understand the seriousness of the situation.

Under Hansen's management the company lost money for two years in a row in a restructuring effort, and then, in the third year, 2002, lost a whopping $84 million. He authorized the purchase of two major distributors and moved the company's headquarters from one city to another. It seemed he was trying to do too much, with an approach that frequently changed direction over two or three years.

Hansen had experienced a substantial amount of success early on at Fleming, and he was responsible for bringing in the Kmart business, but now a different strategy was needed to pull it out of the weeds. The truth was in the numbers. The company was not stable, but Hansen was unwilling to admit it to himself or anyone else, so he did the only thing he knew how to do, which was to act optimistically. The only problem with that was that there was no reason to be optimistic! Maybe he didn't quite understand it all himself, or maybe his team didn't comprehend the impact that losing their largest customer would have on them, but as a leader it was his responsibility and no one else's to dig deep for the truth until he understood the facts. In business, and especially in a public company, if you can't understand or explain something, you're headed for trouble. If you don't understand something, you're on your way toward violating the first principle of transparency without even knowing it. How can you tell the whole truth, if you're not even sure what the truth is? If you're a transparent leader, ignorance isn't an excuse. You have to know your business, you have to be accountable for it, and you have to build it with straight talk and openness.

I've served on several corporate boards in my career and have seen a few other CEOs fall into the same trap. They find it hard to be completely open and honest about the things that aren't going well, and they don't realize that when businesses falter, you have to do the best you can to fix the problem while keeping your shareholders, your board, and your employees fully informed. It's important to take your medicine and get back to doing the right thing, because concealing the truth, or even parts of it, will only get you into deeper trouble.

Another leader who learned this the hard way was former American Airlines CEO Don Carty. Carty was a friendly, approachable executive who had nothing to lose, following, as he did, in the footsteps of Robert Crandall, the tough-as-nails, chain-smoking CEO who often clashed with American's unions.

When Carty took over as CEO in 1998, he quickly became known as a fair and competent leader who managed to steer American through the most turbulent time in aviation history after the terrorist attacks in New York on September 11, 2001. On that dark day the world of air transportation came to a screeching halt. Airports were shut down and planes were grounded, resulting in millions of dollars in losses for the airlines. In the year that followed, air travel slowed to a crawl, corporations imposed moratoriums on business travel, and trips to international destinations sharply declined. The world political climate was tense and it was a difficult time for all companies, but American bled until it barely had any life left in it. The company was losing $5 million a day when Don Carty petitioned Congress for governmental assistance, which the government denied. Five million dollars a day—that's a lot of Dial soap!

Carty probably lost countless nights of sleep as he struggled to find ways to revive a company that had been severely impacted by world events. The economy was sluggish; Americans were falling deep in debt and less apt to have discretionary income to spend on leisure travel, not to mention the fear that many had of getting on an airplane. Road trips replaced annual airline destination vacations, as Americans simply stayed closer to home. In early 2003, when we entered into war with Iraq, the airlines suffered another serious blow.

With the situation rapidly deteriorating, Carty entered into negotiations with American's unions, asking the pilots, flight attendants, and other employees to agree to salary cutbacks to spare the airline from having to file for bankruptcy. After a series of complex negotiations, the unions came to a monumental decision and agreed to $1.8 billion in wage concessions.

For a moment, it seemed that Carty had taken heroic steps and pulled off the impossible. The announcement of the agreement lifted American's shares by 43 percent and Carty praised union leaders, saying their ground-breaking agreements showed "the spirit and the determination and commitment that helped make American the number-one airline in the world and serve notice that we intend to keep that distinction."

Carty, who himself had taken a pay freeze for the two years prior, said all the right things. He announced that he would cut his half-a-million-dollar salary by a third, decline a bonus for the third straight year, and ask the AMR Corporation (parent company of American) board to reduce the compensation of other senior officers. But shortly after this announcement was made, another story emerged. A filing with the Securities and Exchange Commission revealed that the airline had partially funded a supplemental pension trust for forty-five top executives to protect some of their benefits in the event of bankruptcy, and that they had already offered six senior executives, Don Carty included, retention bonuses equal to twice their base salaries. When union members found out, they were furious.

Carty had made a single but career-defining error. He hadn't been open, even though the executive bonuses could have been explained and justified. A company spokesman defended them later, explaining that they were, in fact, not unlike measures taken to protect pilots' pensions, but by then it was too late, and when news of the compensation leaked out, it sealed the CEO's fate. The unions were enraged, shares of AMR plummeted, and the board acted swiftly to vote him out the following week. What a shame!

PRINCIPLE NUMBER 2:
BUILD A VALUES-BASED CULTURE

Can corporations instill values? It's a radical notion, when you consider that we're programmed early on to keep our business and personal lives separate. In addition, building a corporate culture from the ground up or changing one that's flawed can seem overwhelming. Values are inherently personal, but they *can* be acquired, and some companies have proven that a values-based culture can increase the bottom line.

I knew this was the direction we needed to go to succeed at Dial, but there were a lot of potholes preventing an employee-friendly culture. I had to start by being open with employees about my intention to create a different business environment, so senior management went off on a retreat to create what we now refer to as our "cultural contract," so that everyone—employees, management, and shareholders—would have a stake in the company and make decisions based on a shared value system.

Values are simply a list of things that are important to you, the foundation of "rules" that makes your company tick, but when the employees buy into them, you'll witness massive change. But a lot has to happen to make it succeed. To begin with . . . it takes patience. You have to determine what your corporate mission will be, and you have to clearly define what you stand for.

When I was the chairman and CEO of Quaker State Corporation, we defined our core values with a credo, but we also enforced a financial statement certification process for every business unit to back up our intent to report completely and honestly. This meant that the manager of each business unit was required to sign off on a document that stated that he or she agreed to generally accepted accounting and reporting principles. It was our way of ensuring accuracy in reporting the numbers. Our employees had skin in the game, and it showed that we were serious about integrity—and this was years before the current Sarbanes-Oxley regulations. After all, if management doesn't set the standard for excellence early on, who will? It's important to create that point of reference and communicate it clearly from day one, and reiterate it again and again. Your values shouldn't change, regardless of how the rest of the business universe outside your company behaves.

I've found that getting core values into every nook and cranny of a company is an ongoing process, and not one to take lightly. You have to be engaged in it, but you also have to be willing to identify those employees with mind-sets that are contrary to the culture, and either change their conflicting philosophies or create an exit strategy to move them out of your company. If the head of your purchasing department, for instance, doesn't share the same values as the rest of the company, your relationships with vendors may be based on the wrong things. You may have billing discrepancies, miscommunications, or a relationship with a person or company who makes compromises that will eventually have a negative impact on your business.

Defining Values: Who Are We and What Do We Stand For?

At Dial, I knew early on that the first step toward a turnaround would have to be to turn the corporate culture into one that was values-based. We had to get the management team to buy in, so we started at the top, by taking a team of the top twenty-three executives to a mountain getaway in Sedona, Arizona. The goal was to spend three solid days together away from the distractions of the office, email, and phone calls; to get to know each other and brainstorm until we could create a new vision for the company. These were the highest levels of management in the company—officers and the key managers representing most departments—and we had sessions where we heard everyone's thoughts on strategy, values, and operating principles. Each of us talked about the high and low points in our lives, and how we dealt with them. In a way, we became a family, and you could hear the big, oozing sound of politics leaving our culture. In between sessions, there was a series of physical activities facilitated by a company that specializes in team building. Employees navigated a course of rope climbing and learned about trust, and the value of being close knit with their colleagues. In the end, there were a lot of great ideas for moving forward, and we had a foundation for establishing a new corporate culture.

When we returned to the office, the leadership team decided to share the cultural contract with all employees to build individual commitment to our new operating philosophy. The hope was that if management acted as the role models and embraced the new philosophy, the entire company would take the cue to act accordingly.

One employee who attended the Sedona team-building session, Mary Jane Harris, Dial's vice president of manufacturing, was ultimately promoted to senior vice president of human resources—the department that now "owns" the cultural contract. Because she was involved from day one, she understood how to keep the cultural contract and its principles alive, and how to best implement it with new employees as they came on board. It was a long process, but eventually every single employee willingly signed the contract, and we had it printed on the back of our business cards to show others our commitment to it.

I realize that nowadays a cultural contract is no big deal. It's the "in" thing to do, but we did it long before it was fashionable, simply because we needed to clearly communicate our values and ideas about the way we wanted everyone in the organization to conduct business. Today, after a potential new hire reads the cultural contract, the hiring manager talks about it with them, which gives both the manager and the potential employee the chance to see if they'll be a good fit. If someone doesn't agree with our culture, no matter how good they are at what they do, we know they're not going to mesh well within our company. Of course most people trying to get you to hire them aren't going to talk your company down or disagree with the way you're running it, but the discussion is a good one, because it gives people the opportunity to ask pointed questions about the way someone would make decisions. We do this from day one, and it's not just a bunch of stuff we created just so we can say we do it.

Getting Started: Define Your Culture

Some of the most successful people I know have worked hard in their careers to promote values-based cultures. That's because they understand that defining your mission, your vision, and your culture, is a key ingredient in long-term success and sustainable profits.

The first step in the process of creating a transparent organization is to define it in writing. Once it's set in black and white, you'll have the road map you need to move forward. A cultural mission statement helps you communicate your core values in a way that's not preachy or imposing, and if the employees help create it, it becomes a lifestyle rather than a mandate from above.

While it sounds pretty basic, the Dial Corporation's cultural contract states:

- We treat everyone with dignity and respect.
- We are open and honest with each other.
- We develop and leverage the abilities and perspectives of all individuals in our diverse organization.
- We involve the right people in making decisions and base them on what is best for the entire company.
- We make decisions taking into account both the short-term and long-term needs of the company.
- We set challenging, realistic goals and deliver on our commitments.
- We encourage and reward initiative and risk-taking.
- We regularly communicate with each other on important issues and developments.
- We require and demonstrate ethical behavior and integrity in all our business interactions at every level in the organization.

Imagine how great life would be if every relationship were based on these same nine principles! But you have to take it further. Once you've *defined* the right culture for your company, you have to take action to write it, promote it, and live it. Then you can't back down.

Implementing the Defined Culture: What Comes Next?

The truth is, defining what you are or who you want to be as an organization is easy. The hard part is taking the action required to achieve it. Defining your corporate culture is phase one, and it's a significant step, but the most important part of building a values-based culture is phase two: implementation.

Implementing a corporate culture, whether you're building it from the ground up or changing an existing one, involves continual communication to reinforce your message. How do you want your employees to act? What rules should they follow? How should they make their decisions? How will truth, integrity, and values-based decisions help our business? What's the leader's position on these issues? All of these subjects need to be addressed on a consistent, on-going basis.

When we bring on a new hire at Dial, we continue the process of open communication about our culture by giving them total access to senior management. This builds transparency. Each and every employee—regardless of their stature, salary, or position—has the same access to me and my management team. I tell everyone to email me, to call, or even to come and see me, and believe me, they do. I respond to every email myself, and as soon as I hit "reply," the pen pal phenomenon kicks in and that initial response gives them a level of comfort that generates an email anytime there's something on their mind. Most employees feel comfortable writing to me, and I get emails and phone calls about everything you can imagine. This type of empowerment and openness prevents pockets of exclusion, and it avoids nasty surprises such as a manager who mistreats employees, because eventually someone would let me know. Transparent leadership fosters a culture of integrity, accountability, and openness.

PRINCIPLE NUMBER 3: HIRE "PEOPLE PEOPLE"

How do the people you work with affect the overall value of a company? The answer is easy: people are the number-one asset in any company, and how good they are directly affects shareholder value. Jack Welch, the former CEO of General Electric, told me that the executive he relies on the most is the head of Human Resources, who always knows what's going on with the *people* in the organization. The third principle of creating a transparent organization involves looking for specific character traits in the employees you hire and develop in order to create the transparent business culture. "People people" are the service-providers, and they're the kind of employees who not only understand the importance of good service, but they also truly want to be team players. They're genuinely good people, and as a result they work from a foundation of integrity. They make honest decisions, and they strive to serve the customer's needs and be as good at what they do as they can be. *And* they are critical to any transparent organization's success!

If you're turning a company around or just trying to make one better, you have to first understand the value of the employee personalities who will have the most to offer your team.

The transparent employee is a people person. They're people who relate well to others, and they tend to be genuinely nice and helpful. But most importantly, they tell the truth. They work for the organization rather than for themselves. The concept of providing service isn't beneath them. They know the customer comes first. "People people" can make a company soar, and their personalities can attract new customers and suppliers that otherwise wouldn't have been interested in your company.

I've found that interpersonal skills are just as important as the facts and achievements found on someone's résumé. This may seem like a foreign concept in an era where corporations use computer programs to sift through résumés for words that fit specific job descriptions. But consider this: technology can find the hard skills, like an MBA or a background in engineering, but it can't find the soft skills—qualities such as innovation, someone who thinks service and integrity are important, and people who like other people. These are the people who make an organization sing. It's these employees who will embrace the idea of transparency because they will make decisions from a foundation of values, and work by the standards you have set for the corporate culture. Their inherent goodness, along with their skills and talents, will make them the best candidates for leading your company to success.

THE ROAD TO TRANSPARENCY

Every values-based corporate culture has a leader employees can reach. The culture is one of accessibility, and the employees in those companies know they can voice their views, even to the CEO if they want to.

The road to transparency is itself an open one—it's not a traffic jam of corporate politics, where the CEO resides in an ivory tower.

Believe it or not, there are still some companies where the CEO works in a special office on the highest floor of the building that only those with a secret pass code or key can access. If you're the CFO, you probably have the key. If you're the VP of human resources, you might have it, too. But the other employees don't, and even if they did actually find a way onto the executive floor they'd be stopped by a glass wall, and an oversized, intimidating receptionist's desk much bigger than their own. The employee is likely to be treated as a nuisance, because after all, no one gets in to see HIM without first passing through HER. Sound ridiculous? Don't laugh. In some companies this really is the case.

In a transparent company, the CEO is as accessible as he or she can possibly be. Having an office on the same floor as the other employees is important; and he or she will walk the halls, answers employee emails, and be *visible*. At Dial, an employee who works at our soap plant in Illinois has as much access to me as our CFO (an officer of the company whose office is close to mine). That's unheard of in a lot of companies, especially those that are household names, but it's critical to our success. It's important to do that to keep your culture open!

In other companies, a lot of the employees never even get to meet the CEO, and have no idea what he or she is like because the CEO has a reserved parking space, and a special executive dining room where he has lunch with other company executives. Of course the size of a company sometimes limits a CEO's accessibility, but a lot of times that's just an excuse. Accessibility is an attitude that goes a long way in shaping the corporate culture.

I park my VW Beetle in the same employee parking lot everyone else uses, and I have my morning coffee in the employee cafeteria every morning. If I leave my office at midday for a meeting and return to a full parking lot, I have to take the best spot I can find and hike across the hot asphalt to the building, just like anyone else. I'm not better than anyone else, or more important, so why should I have a better parking spot? I'm accessible, and we've defined our culture as an open one.

Tools for Building the Transparent Company

I stress actual physical accessibility as a tool to develop our culture, but there are other means you can use to get the message out. Technology is one of them, and even though changes in technology have created a lot of challenges by giving employees access to things like the Internet and the freedom and danger it brings, it's also opened up the way you can reach and teach. Email is a technology commonly used to communicate everything from a sales meeting to a birthday, but it can also be used to communicate values across a broad employee base frequently and cost-effectively. It's a fast way to send a message, and to reinforce training issues that employees have already received. Sounds simple, but sometimes the best things are. Communication plays a major role in promoting a transparent culture, and doing it frequently is important.

Another thing we do with technology at Dial is to use it to communicate, teach, and educate. We've implemented a Web-based course called "Doing Business with Integrity" that helps us reinforce our commitment to a values-based culture, and it's mandatory for everyone. Home-based employees can access it via the Internet, and anyone at the office can access it from their desktop. Who knew that integrity could be learned at a desktop monitor! There's more to it than that, of course, but the Web-based class is a great way to get the message out. It trains employees how to handle ethical dilemmas by using role playing in real-life scenarios, and it outlines their personal responsibilities and tells them how to report potential violations. In a world where technology reigns, we teach on their terms, which is really the best way to reach some of the younger employees. It's a great course, and by requiring it we're letting them know that we want them to make the *right* choice even when another choice looks like it might benefit Dial. We use whatever methods of communication we can, but we're consistent with the message that achieving results questionably or unethically won't be tolerated.

We also use the Web quite a bit to reinforce messages, via our intranet and employee newsletters, and we also use something we call a "desk drop," which is a more personal approach. We'll desk-drop new products, a letter from me, or anything else that we want to be more personal and individual than an email. We'll take the time to drop a package containing a new Dial product off at every desk, a nice surprise for the employee who gets a gift when he or she returns from lunch! It's personal and it's effective.

In conclusion, I always try to remember how important transparency is to the success of a business culture, and even today, before we hire someone at Dial, we expose them to our core values by showing them our cultural contract during the job interview. Our cultural contract is similar to the ones I've promoted within other companies I've led, but it's unique to Dial because it was created by Dial employees.

Easy, right? Hardly. I haven't fooled myself into thinking that a cultural contract, an online educational program, or even a corporate governance manager are silver bullets that will keep us on track for our integrity goals. It's a continual process of learning and growing.

When I retired from the Midas board of directors, my colleagues gave me a standing ovation, and a few of them even said some nice things about me. Dr. Archie Dykes, a highly rated professional director and the lead director for Pepsi-Americas, was also on the Midas board. I remember Archie saying, "Herb has the ability to cut through the issues and tell it like it is." I remembered those words because if I look back at what I'd like to be recognized for, it's not that I was the CEO of some big corporation. It's that I was an honest person with no hidden agenda.

CHAPTER TWO

THE TRANSPARENT LEADER

Are you a transparent leader?

Every year, management consultants and business-book gurus churn out volumes on the subject of leadership, and if you read them you'd think that being a leader involved detailed graphs and charts, or complex formulas. The truth is a whole lot simpler. The truth is that anyone can develop leadership skills—but it takes a special person to lead *transparently.*

You don't have to look far for examples of mediocre, incompetent, or even deceitful individuals who managed to climb the corporate ladder to rise to leadership positions. The point is that anyone can be a leader, but it takes a unique individual to be a transparent leader.

THE AVERAGE LEADER vs.
THE ABOVE-AVERAGE LEADER

In the past decade the world has seen a number of corporate executives, government officials, and high-profile leaders tripped up by their own mistakes. Some of them even had long runs of success . . . until bad personal decisions caught up with them.

One person who faced this situation was Mike Price, not a high-ranking corporate official but a highly qualified football coach who had led Washington State University to consecutive ten-win seasons, followed by a trip to the Rose Bowl. Price was

example

then hired by the University of Alabama to be Alabama's sixth head coach since the legendary Paul "Bear" Bryant, who was known for his high morals and lofty expectations of players.

Just about everyone knows about Bear Bryant, who set the standard at Alabama with his philosophy that building good character was a fundamental element in building a great team. Bryant was far from an average leader, and Price had big shoes to fill, and he was given a great opportunity that few others would ever have.

Included in Price's seven-year, $10 million contract was a clause that reflected the university's high standards and expectations. The clause said that as coach, he could be fired for *any behavior that brings the employee into public disrepute, contempt, scandal, or ridicule or that reflects unfavorably upon the reputation or the high moral or ethical standards of the university.*

Unfortunately, Mike Price never coached one game for Alabama. University president Robert Witt, the man who had hired him, fired Price after reports emerged that the fifty-seven-year-old coach had spent hundreds of dollars at a topless bar on a trip to Florida, where he was participating in a pro-am golf tournament. The next morning, a woman allegedly in Price's room, ordered nearly a thousand dollars worth of room service and charged it to his hotel bill.

Illegal? No. Bad judgment? Yes. Mike Price's bad judgment impacted his opportunity to enjoy a great coaching job at the venerable University of Alabama, and it also affected his marrige, as well as the careers and reputations of his two sons, whom he had hired to work with him on Alabama's coaching staff. After Witt announced the firing, Price was tearful, but he was also defiant. When he spoke to an auditorium packed with reporters and fans, he criticized the university president for his decision, insisting he deserved a second chance. Price should have been transparent. He should have fessed up and just admitted that he had made a huge error in judgment, and he should have also come clean and said that his own values probably just didn't fit with the Alabama organization. The whole incident was something that the university could have ignored because it happened off campus, before the football season started. It didn't involve the school, it involved only Price's personal life. But Robert Witt wasn't willing to settle for good enough, and he wasn't interested in having an organization based on mediocre values. In explaining his decision to terminate the coach to the media, President Witt called Price a great coach and a good man but said that he failed to live his personal and professional life in a manner consistent with university policies. That was it; the end. Transparency, leadership, and courage exemplified.

Witt did a good job of preventing a roadblock that could have inhibited the culture of integrity Alabama wanted to maintain. What kind of message would it send to the future generation of football players if the university had kept the coach? The university president stood his ground. He didn't cave in to pressures to reinstate the fired football coach.

Intolerance for bad personal behavior is rare to find, but Witt handled the situation the way he thought he should, based on his own value system. He made an unpopular decision to fire a popular coach whom players admired. He was criticized by some for making a mountain out of a molehill, but in the long run it would prove to be a decision that would establish an expectation for future performance for those representing the university.

Robert Witt is not an average leader. A lot of people would have been tempted to cave in to pressure to forgive the transgression and keep the newly hired coach, which would have avoided the difficult task of going through a time-consuming search for another coach. But Witt had already established his core values and expectations, and they were clearly outlined in the coaches' employment contract. He had high standards and he wasn't about to let any obstacle stand in the way. Being a good leader means doing business honestly, ethically, and transparently, and it's as simple as that. It doesn't mean producing stellar results by compromising values.

What Kind of Leader Are You?

A survey found that 90 percent of Americans think that they're smarter than the average person. It's true that most people think of themselves as more cunning and brighter than the next person; yet it's the minority that truly breaks out of the mold of mediocrity to achieve excellence at anything. What kind of leader are *you*?

You can be average, or you can make the decision to be more than that. But there aren't any magical formulas or secret handshakes that gain you entry into any Great Leaders Club of America. Good leadership is a learned *skill,* and you have to work hard at it. It means being an open person, and doing business as if everything you say or do will end up on the front page of the local newspaper.

In his book *Good to Great,* author Jim Collins describes the ultimate leader as a "Level 5," a leader who, among other things, is "modest and willful, humble and fearless." Other business books describe leadership in terms of strategy, outlining how to go about creating an action plan to get the best results. In the widely acclaimed book *Execution,* by Larry Bossidy, a great leader executes, by developing seven essential behaviors, including "follow through," and "reward the doers," and in the best-selling book *Thriving on Chaos,* author Tom Peters describes great leaders as lovers of change.

Confused? The bottom line is that there are a lot of different theories on what it takes to be a leader, but the barometer of true success is transparency. It's not how strong the numbers are (because success hinges on *how* you achieved them), and it's not how aggressive the sales team is. If you're not transparent, it doesn't matter if you're a good executor, if you're modest or fearless, or even if you're the most charismatic, chaos-loving leader around. What matters is whether you can look in the mirror and see a true reflection, and be glad that you got up in the morning to play the game with honesty and integrity.

In *Good to Great,* Collins details the five-year process his research team went through to understand why some companies make the leap to greatness and others don't. What they discovered was that instead of setting strategy first, the leaders of those companies "First get the right people on the bus, the wrong people off the bus, and the right people in the right seats. Then, they figure out where to drive it." It's a simple concept—hire great people and you'll have great employees—but it's not new. Effective leaders have been using it for years, and it's a big part of leading transparently. Great employees are open, honest, and will make values-based decisions that end up benefiting the entire company. But transparency takes the good-to-great concept a bit further.

In addition to becoming great, companies should strive to become *transparent,* which transcends greatness. This is something a lot of leaders have missed by buying into one trend or another and overlooking the importance of integrity as a goal and a performance target. All of those business strategies in the books could be true, but again, it really won't matter if you're an executor, a lover of change, or a Level 5 if you and your employees aren't totally honest. Transparency—the art of being open and honest about all things—is mandatory for sustained success.

So, back to the question I posed at the beginning of the chapter: Are you a transparent leader? If you're not sure, maybe you could use a little tune-up. Take the transparency test, below; answer each question yes or no.

The transparency test:

1. Have you ever hidden a mistake from a superior or a colleague?
2. Have you ever failed to disclose a product bug, defect, shortcoming, or something else to a customer, or told a customer something that wasn't entirely true to win their business?
3. Have you ever expensed a lunch or dinner, or office supplies, when it wasn't exclusively for business?
4. Does your organization have a written cultural contract?
5. Can you list all of the items on the contract right now, without reading it?
6. Are you accessible to every employee you manage, and if you're a CEO, to every employee in the company?
7. Do you admit mistakes in your department (or company) and report them publicly?
8. Do you encourage whistle-blowers?

Some of the questions are easier to answer than others, but if any of them make you cringe, your transparency needs work. (A transparent leader would have answered no to the first three and yes to the rest of the questions on the list.)

Do You Make More Than You're Worth?

Just a few weeks after the terrorists struck the World Trade Center on September 11, 2001, I gave a speech to the students and faculty of Thunderbird University in Phoenix, Arizona. Thunderbird, the American Graduate School of International Management, was ranked number one in international business education by *U.S. News & World Report* for eight consecutive years, and number one in the *Wall Street Journal*'s inaugural business-school ranking. Thunderbird's executive education programs are recognized as among the world's best, and the school is known for having a diverse and global faculty. Several of the professors were born, raised, and educated outside the United States, and the student population represents more than eighty nations. It's a great school.

By the time I was scheduled to give my speech at Thunderbird, the Enron scandal had already hit the papers and the headlines teemed with stories about corrupt executives and unscrupulous CEOs. As I looked out over the podium at the faces before me, it was a very different feeling I had than the proud feeling of achievement I'd experienced in the past as a CEO addressing a group of future leaders of America. I became suddenly aware of the negative perception these students— and nearly everyone in America—had of corporate leaders. For a moment I felt like Bill Clinton addressing a group of feminists.

I hadn't done anything wrong, but I knew I would be painted with the same brush as every bad executive who had appeared lately in the media. I said something to the effect of: "I'd like to tell you that I'm a firefighter, or a teacher, but I'm not. I'm Herb Baum, and I'm the CEO of a public company."

In that year and in the years since, there has been a lot of disillusionment with the leaders of public companies that centered on scandal and the exorbitant pay packages they were receiving. I use the term *leader* lightly, because some of these executives weren't really acting like leaders—taking huge payouts while driving their own companies into the ground.

During the war in Iraq, the U.S. economy was in a downward spiral and corporate America was in a crisis. Retirement funds were losing value by the day, and the average worker had to rethink their investment strategy and future, making changes like taking an extra job for the income that would put their kids through college, or sending the stay-at-home mom back to work. There were huge layoffs, yet some executives didn't feel as if *they* should be impacted at all. An October 2003 article in the *Wall Street Journal* reported that executive pay was still on the rise, and was expected to increase in the years to come. It didn't seem to matter that everyone else was struggling. The article reported that the CEOs continued to find creative compensation methods to bulk up their salaries without it showing up in the base pay.

All of this led *Fortune* magazine to publish an unprecedented cover depicting an executive in a suit with a pig's head, and an accompanying article about exorbitant pay. You would think all of that scrutiny would lead to some real change. Yet a year and a half later, Dick Grasso, the chairman of the New York Stock Exchange, was forced to resign over the same issue. His pay had grown to excessive levels, and when Grasso's $139.5 million pay package was made public, a groundswell of irate people called for his resignation. Investors, fund managers, and politicians joined the fray, even though Grasso had been at the exchange for thirty-six years and had established a solid reputation as a good leader.

Grasso had worked hard to rise to chairman, starting from the position of clerk. He was successful at what he did, and he was paid a $5 million bonus for navigating the exchange through the events of September 11th. Grasso was rewarded for his performance by a compensation committee of respected business leaders, and it seemed as if he had done everything the right way. So why was his career undone over a single issue—compensation? I guess some would say that Grasso was in the wrong place at the wrong time, when compensation was being scrutinized. But it makes a good case for transparency, and for understanding the value of what you're worth and the job you're being paid for. In the end, Grasso was said to be indifferent about the attention his pay was receiving.

I met Grasso several times, and I've sat next to him at lunch in the NYSE boardroom. He seemed quite competent, but we all know competence isn't enough. His excellent leadership skills in running the NYSE were overshadowed by what appeared to be a huge compensation package. Why are we so worried about big job executive pay, when a .250 hitting major league second baseman makes more than the president of the United States? Everything needs to be judged against performance and the size of the job. Period.

Executive compensation is one of the most important pieces of transparency because it's the catalyst for so many other things. It can cause CEOs to cut corners or do the wrong thing. If a CEO is grossly overpaid compared to company performance, it can lead to pressure in other areas to manipulate financial reporting to make the company's numbers look better overall. That's a no-win situation. And if a CEO is profiting while his or her company is losing money year after year and employees are being laid off, it's just plain wrong to take a bonus. A lot of the skill involved in leading transparently is about developing good judgment to make wise decisions.

There can't be any separation between being a transparent leader and being a transparent person, because people who conduct their personal lives openly and honestly will act the same way in a business situation. The Grasso situation is a perfect lesson for those striving for transparency because it doesn't matter if you're competent, excellent at what you do, or tenured—you have to be transparent, open, and fair. To be the best leader, you have to have a clear and honest concept of your value, your contribution to the organization, and how much that's worth. It means having enough integrity to make the hard decisions, even if it involves reducing your own compensation when everyone is telling you you're worth a thousand times more than your highest-paid employee.

TRANSPARENCY TAKES COURAGE

Sometimes transparency hurts—I can't put it any simpler than that. As a board member who has had to vote out a CEO a few times, it is not only painful for all concerned but sad . . . very sad. That's because failure is never recognized early enough, and the first thing that enters your mind is *give him one more chance.* It's human nature to want to give someone the benefit of the doubt, but when it comes to things like integrity, you can't afford to.

When it comes to being a board member, I've learned that where there's smoke, there's usually a blazing building. So, as tough as it is to vote out a friend or trusted colleague, you just have to do it and get on with what's best for the business.

If you're transparent, you've had to make some hard decisions, and that takes courage. You've had to tell it like it is more than once, and you've been faced with people who don't agree with your point of view. If you're transparent, you've been courageous at times to make decisions based on what's right, and it hasn't always been easy. This is important to realize, because transparency isn't a trend—it's a process, and an evolution.

At Dial, our employees never have to guess where I stand on an issue. I don't believe it would be beneficial to mince words or communicate in flowery prose when I can tell it like it is and say what I mean. I defined our goals from day one, and I was pretty clear about our vision. As we evolved, I always let everyone know what's going on.

When I first joined Dial, I said that it would be in the best interest of shareowners if Dial were part of a larger company. When employees heard what I said, I wasn't the most popular guy on the block. Who wants to hear the new guy in charge say that the company has a for sale sign on it? They reacted the way most would, with fear and skepticism. But it was the truth, and I wasn't going to tell it any other way. Most of all, it was important that they hear it from me rather than the newspapers, television, or the rumor mill. I told them that the absolute best option for shareholders and employees would be to sell the company at a price that would increase the value of the stock and therefore increase the value of their retirement accounts as well. Being upfront and out there isn't always the easiest thing to do, but it's the right thing to do.

•   •   •

Shortly after my appointment as the new CEO of Dial, I received a phone call while I was in London on vacation from Reuben Mark, the chairman and CEO of Colgate-Palmolive, a major competitor. Colgate competes directly with Dial in several market segments and often comes out on top. I have a lot of respect for the company and I knew Reuben to be an outstanding CEO with an excellent reputation. The day he called, he said that he had in his possession a CD containing Dial Soap's marketing plan for the year. It had been given to him by a member of his sales force (a former Dial employee who had taken it with him when he left to join Colgate), and it meant that one of Dial's most important product line's strategies had been revealed, and could result in the loss of revenue, profits, and market share.

"Herb," Reuben said, "one of our new salespeople gave this CD to one of my sales managers. I'm not going to look at this information, and I'm sending it back to you right now. I'll handle it on this end."

It was the clearest case of leading with honor and transparency I've witnessed in my career. After all, who expects a CEO to call his competitor and tell him they have a copy of their detailed business strategy? If he hadn't, I never would have known, but that one call gave me more insight into his character than anything else. It wasn't hard to see why he had been so successful in his career. He knew he didn't need to gain an unfair competitive advantage to succeed, even when he was presented with the opportunity. He chose not to abandon his leadership style, and he had the courage to stick to his principles even when it meant giving up confidential information that could have helped his company gain an edge. Transparency takes courage.

The Critical Difference

This brings us back to the critical difference between average leaders and the above-average ones. Transparent leaders *think about integrity*. They're thinking about integrity all the time, and anticipating what should and shouldn't be within the framework of integrity. They're anticipating their next move, the company's next move, and what's best for their employees. They're asking themselves a lot of questions—and guess what?

Sometimes the answers aren't pleasing. Am I honest about everything? Are we doing things fairly? Do I make too much money? That's a critical difference between an average leader and a transparent one.

I've had to ask myself that last question before, and it led me to make a request to the Dial board of directors that would have allowed me to divide up a portion of my bonus to the company's lowest-paid employee group. I did it because I personally feel that executive pay is out of control, and that a lot of CEOs, including me, are overpaid.

In 2002, my second year at Dial, we met our goals and exceeded everyone's expectations, so I asked the board if I could forgo a portion of my bonus to give more to the entry-level folks. I didn't want it going to the executives, who were already making a good amount of money; I wanted it to go to the people who made the least amount of money at the company. These were people who played a significant but unsung role in our success, yet I thought they were probably struggling to make ends meet in their own households. They had kids to support, groceries to buy, and house payments to make. The board met about the request and ultimately agreed to provide additional funds to allow for the incremental bonuses to be given. We were able to pay out thousands of dollars to some employees, and it was found money that they didn't know they'd be getting! It made me feel good to be able to surprise them like that, because they played an important role in the company's new success.

It all happened at a time when high-level executives at a lot of other companies were taking big payoffs for themselves, and I really think it contributed to building the values Dial has today. Dial's turnover rate is the lowest it's been in eleven years! I received a lot of letters thanking me for their bonuses, and some of them were from employees who said something like that had never happened to them. One told me, "Now I'll be able to do more for my kids." I got a great deal of satisfaction out of that.

THE DUTIES OF A TRANSPARENT LEADER

I've been around some good leaders and some not-so-good ones in my career, and the good ones know that the only way to develop an integrity-based workforce is to work hard at it. They know that if their employees are afraid of the consequences of what might happen if they make a simple mistake that they'll be tempted to cover up mistakes. They also know that an open culture, where employees can admit their problems and talk about mistakes, develops employees who are less tempted to sweep things under the rug for you to find later on, after significant damage has been done.

A Transparent Leader Must Cultivate Integrity

Personal development is a big part of cultivating integrity in every company, because any time you have a lot of different personalities and backgrounds, you're going to have challenges. People make mistakes, and you shouldn't fire them all when they do! You owe it to your employees, in some cases anyway, to give them at least one chance to fix things, because there might be other stressors going on at home or somewhere in that person's life that's causing the behavior. That's why employee assistance programs are so effective. They help employees get treatment or counseling for their personal problems in a safe and nonthreatening way.

If you find that one of your employees hasn't demonstrated integrity or has lied about something, you'll have to examine whether or not the behavior that led to the lie in the first place can be reformed, or whether the lie itself is a behavior that can negatively impact your business. In the end, hopefully you'll be remembered as an ethical leader who helped people through troubled waters, rather than a ruthless one who watched them go under when they tipped the canoe.

A Transparent Leader Must Listen

Sometimes it's hard to be a good listener. We're human, after all, and we're not like dogs or cats that have senses so heightened that they can hear even the lowest-frequency sounds without effort. Some animals run in erratic circles when an earthquake is about to hit because they can hear the P waves, the very first pressure waves at the rupturing fault of an earthquake; but a lot of times we humans don't know a disaster is coming until it's too late. Wouldn't it be nice if you could sense every disaster at the rupturing fault, before it hit your life or business? But we're human, and it's not that easy. We have to work on developing our listening skills, and we have to think of listening as an important component of leading.

Listening is especially important for leaders at high levels. If you want the truth, you have to get into the trenches and listen; otherwise the information you receive will be filtered up through employees and managers until it reaches you clean, clear, and . . . distorted. You won't hear about the issues that negatively impact your business units, you won't hear about the employee who made your customer angry, and you won't hear about the demeaning manager who affects employee productivity (negatively). If you make it a point to listen at every level and keep an open-door policy that encourages employees to communicate with you, you'll be able to hear the good and the bad, and detect disasters before they strike. Be a good listener. You'll be surprised how much you'll learn.

As a CEO, I know that when I'm called to attend an employee or management meeting within our company, there have already been meetings before the meeting. If I'm due to attend a sales meeting, I know that the sales team has met beforehand to talk about what will happen at the meeting I've been invited to attend. If I'm scheduled for a plant visit, I know that the plant employees have been prepped, and meetings have been held to talk about the image they want to project when I get there. On several plant visits, the walls had been freshly painted for my arrival! I know I'm getting clean, filtered information at these scheduled meetings, and I know that I've really got to listen to everything else that's going on to get the whole truth.

When I started at Dial I wanted to create an open atmosphere where employees felt they could say whatever was on their minds. It was important for our growth, and also because the company had been led by someone else with a different philosophy and management style. When you take a stand and decide to have an open management style, you have to be willing to listen to everything and accept the good feedback along with the bad, because not everyone will have compliments and great revenue-generating ideas to send your way. I was ready for it, and sure enough the emails and other messages came.

One morning I arrived in my office to find an email from an employee who wanted to inform me of a problem.

SENT: Wednesday, March 20, 2002, 2:46 PM
TO: Baum, Herbert
SUBJECT:

I know that you are a busy man, and that this may seem like something petty, but for the past 3 weeks, there has been a dead bird laying on the lawn outside the stairwell at the south end of the building facing the front of the building.

I went to one of the supervisors in CIC and she said not to worry about it, that lawn maintenance would remove it. I waited patiently for the lawn people to arrive and went out on my break that day to smoke and saw that the bird was still there. I again approached the supervisor that I spoke to and she stated that she would email or call someone else about it.

I just wanted to let you know that the bird is still out there, decomposing on the lawn.

I am not an animal activist or anything like that but someone who cares about everything. I keep thinking, this was a wild animal that could have any number of diseases and no telling what kind of bugs. And for it to be decomposing like that, it cannot be too healthy for the people that are downstairs smoking.

I spoke to another supervisor about this and she asked me why it was bothering me so much. I told her that I was not sure, but it just did not seem right, that it should have been taken care of by now. I have been tempted to spend my 30 minute lunch break on walking around the building with a trash bag and picking it up myself, but do not feel that is my job to do.

I am not complaining on the first supervisor that I spoke to. She did try to get this taken care of, but I just thought that you should know, seeing how nothing has been accomplished thus far.

Thank you.

I sent him a simple reply intended to thank him, but I also let him know I'd take action to respond to his concern and solve the problem.

FROM: Baum, Herbert
SENT: Thursday, March 21, 2002, 5:35 AM
SUBJECT: RE:

Thanks for letting me know. I'll have it taken care of first thing this morning.

Herb 3/21/02

Apparently some poor feathered friend had lost his way and flown into the side of our building, and the employee was concerned enough to write me about the health issues the bird carcass could create. Someone asked me afterward if it had crossed my mind to ask him which would be a bigger health concern, smoking or a dead bird, but it never did; anyway, that wasn't my judgment to make. The real issue was that I had received an email from an employee, one of my company's great assets, and that I had to protect that asset and what was important to him. Apparently the dead bird was repugnant to him. I took it seriously, and I went down and found someone from our janitorial staff right away. The bird was cleared away within the hour, and though it might sound like a trivial issue to some, when I had encouraged employees to write to me I didn't say they couldn't write to me about dead birds. I had asked them to write to me about *anything* they wanted to. If you're going to be taken seriously, you have to be serious about your open-door policy and not filter or judge what comes before you. You have to treat each and every employee with respect, even if you don't share their point of view, and even if you consider it a minor issue.

Being accessible is a good way to hone your listening skills, and it also allows you to stay in touch with colleagues and employees. One way I do this is through a program I call "Hot Dogs with Herb." It's a fun, casual lunch where I get to spend quality time with a small group of employees—usually ten to twelve people. It allows them to get to know me, and gives me a chance to get to know them and to listen to their concerns or feedback. We always have hot dogs—my favorite dish—and it gives me time to sit and chat with people to learn what's going on in their life inside the company, and outside too. It's a small thing, but it gives them a chance to ask me questions and to understand how I think about things. There's no agenda; we just sit around and talk about things, from office amenities to our products to where the best place in town for pizza is! It's a great way for me to understand what employees think about different issues and for them to get answers directly from me. It's also great for the corporate culture, because it's real, down to earth, ongoing communication, and it helps discern fact from fiction. If there's a rumor, it can be squashed right away before it has a chance to infect the company.

People can ask me whatever they want during the Hot Dogs with Herb sessions, and they get a straight answer. We solve problems, change policies, and get to know each other, and in the process I work to be a good, accessible leader, a friend, and hopefully even a mentor.

Leading the Leader

When you're a transparent leader who listens to employees, true and positive change occurs. The door is always open, and new ideas are generated and put into action. Some of the best leaders I know are people who really listen to their employees.

During my time as the CEO of Quaker State Corporation, there was an employee who worked at our refinery in Congo, West Virginia, who used to give me a performance review once a year. She was an administrative assistant and she would call once in a while and tell me what, in her opinion, I was doing wrong with the company, and what, if anything, I was doing right. I listened, because I wanted to be accessible and I wanted to learn from whatever she had to say. The transparent leader listens—even when it may not be something he or she really wants to hear.

Listening can give you knowledge that you didn't have before, but it can also reap great rewards when it comes to employee morale, loyalty, and how they feel about being part of the company. I'm always interested in listening to our employees' perspectives on how we're interacting with the customer, and how well we've adopted the core values established in our cultural contract.

In addition, I need to listen directly to the customer to hear the full story, so one day I asked our customer-service people if I could spend time at the consumer center listening in on the incoming calls we receive about our products. At the center, consumers can call in on a toll-free number that's printed on our packaging and offer suggestions or even complaints. We get it all. I listened to some of the calls to get a better understanding of what our consumers were saying about us, and to see how our employees handled it, and it turned out to be such a valuable exercise that I found myself talking about it at an employee meeting. A short time later I received a note from one of our employees in research and development who thought it would be a good idea to extend this concept to other areas of the company. She proposed having people from marketing listen in, and people in her own department and other departments listen in to gain a fresh perspective on how our consumers think. I told her to run with it and make it happen, and she did. The "listen in" program is now another great way for us to let our employees know the importance of listening, which in turn allows us to provide better products to our consumers. Not only did we gain a great program that still works today, we empowered the employee who came up with the idea to implement it. If you care about your employees and listen to them, they'll care about you—and your company will reap the rewards.

A Transparent Leader Abides by the First Principle of Transparency: Tell the Whole Truth

In the Kahlil Gibran classic *The Prophet,* first published in 1923, the author writes; "Say not, I have found the truth, but rather, I have found a truth." It's a good quote because it pretty much sums up all the theories business books have touted about leadership. Everyone has an opinion on leadership, and every opinion is what is believed to be *the* truth at the time. But really, they have not found *the* truth, but *a* truth.

If you're transparent you never have to worry about what leadership strategy or philosophy you're going to follow, and there's great freedom and a higher level of credibility involved when people realize that you're managing a business openly and honestly. When you disclose as much as possible, investors will have confidence in the company and its long-term direction, and analysts will continue to be interested in the facts while they praise you for being totally honest, even when you disclose news that isn't so great.

One of the hardest lessons for someone new to a leadership position to learn is that a great leader isn't just a people pleaser. A great leader is proactive and consistently works to do the right thing.

When you're proactive about doing the right thing, you don't make decisions just to please others. You're focused on telling the whole truth, and because that's your focus, you can learn from others and not get misguided by others who don't do things the right way.

When you strive to tell the whole truth, you have to be honest with yourself, too. I learned that lesson early on when I majored in finance in college to please my father, who was an attorney and tax accountant. My father would have liked to see me follow in his footsteps and take over his neighborhood law and accounting practice, but there was just one problem: I dreaded accounting. I thought it was boring, and still do today. But I majored in finance to prove to him that I could do it, and after graduation from Drake University, I had a short stint in a bank training program in Chicago. It wasn't long before I decided to move away from a career with numbers. Let's face it, most people don't want to balance their own checkbooks, let alone do it for anyone else. I felt the very same way. If I had been true to myself I probably would have majored in marketing instead! But I learned from the experience, and that was the last time I did something I didn't like doing.

You have to be honest with yourself and others about your capabilities before you can lead anyone else. It's a process of growth. I was lucky to have a good comprehension of right and wrong from childhood, but I also benefited from some of the lessons I learned early in my career. I learned from my own experiences, but also from the actions of others, that honesty truly is the only way. It's a lesson that served me well throughout my entire career.

One crucial moment that helped shape my perspective early in my career was when I landed my very first job interview with Aaron Cushman and Associates, an entertainment-oriented public relations firm in Chicago. *The interview* was a big deal for me at the time, because it was with Mr. Cushman himself, in his office on the corner of Michigan Avenue and Wacker Drive. We talked for a while, but Cushman said he didn't have any jobs available, and even if he did, he said, I had no experience. He was right . . . but I really wanted to work for him. I had never worked in public relations, but I knew that I was pretty creative and that all I needed was a chance.

Cushman, staring out the window, pointed to the Wrigley Building across the street. "I need to see if you can write," he said. "I'd like you to do some research and write me a story about the person who turns on the floodlights that illuminate the façade of the Wrigley Building at night."

"Great," I said, eager to take on the challenge. I made a beeline for the Wrigley Building to find the mysterious individual responsible for the lights! There were thousands of lights dotting the Chicago landmark, and I wondered if there was an old man who watched the sky, waiting for it to get dark before he ran in to switch the lights on. But when I did my research, it didn't take long to figure out that the assignment would be more challenging than I thought. I soon discovered that the Wrigley Building lights turned on automatically! No interesting old guy who had been there a hundred years manning his post . . . the Wrigley lights were automatic!

Not to be deterred, I constructed the story as a mystery, and it wasn't until the surprise ending that you learned that it was a machine and not a person that switched on the lights. Cushman must have liked my creativity because he hired me for a small assignment working with a motor speedway on the outskirts of Chicago.

I started right away, and my first day on the job I drove out to the track to meet with the owner, a man by the name of Howard Tiedt who had hired Aaron Cushman Associates to do all of his advertising and public relations. Howard had built a clay track for stock car racing, motorcycle racing, and midget cars. The races held there in the spring and summer packed in the crowds in the town of Willow Springs, Illinois.

"What do you know about racing?" Howard asked.

"Nothing," I replied.

"I'm disappointed. I really wanted someone who knew something about racing. If you don't know anything about racing you can't work on my account."

Once again, my lack of experience presented an obstacle. I walked back to my car feeling defeated, and made the long drive to Aaron Cushman's office to tell him the speedway didn't want me because I didn't know anything about auto racing.

"I don't have any other jobs," Mr. Cushman said, and at that point I knew I had no other option except to drive back to the track again to try and convince Howard to give me a chance. I did, and when I found Howard, I asked him how I could learn the auto racing business. I think I convinced him that I wasn't going to go away anytime soon.

"Maybe you can assist the track announcer," he said. "I'll pay you twenty dollars a night in addition to your job at Cushman and Associates."

I had been pretty shy up to that point and had never done any public speaking, but I seized the opportunity and started working three nights a week at the track helping out the track announcer. That experience opened up a whole new world for me—the world of auto racing. I learned how to describe a race using phrases I had never heard before, like "the cars are so close you can throw a blanket over them!"

After a while I was promoted to the position of track announcer, and I kept that job for thirteen years, even after I joined another advertising and PR firm. Being honest about my lack of experience never turned out to be a deterrent, and it led to the start of an interesting sideline. I had always had positive experiences by being open and honest, and the auto racing experience came in handy when I went to work for Quaker State, a motor oil company that was deeply involved in stock car racing. It prepared me for speaking in front of crowds, which I still do today, and it taught me that sometimes the best jobs are the ones that find you, and that being straight with people is the only way to go.

When you're truthful about your own capabilities it's easy to define the type of culture you want your organization to gravitate toward. Transferring your own business philosophy to the whole team establishes that culture, but first you have to have the foundation that will help define the vision.

A Transparent Leader Learns from the Failures (and Successes) of Others

You can learn a lot by observing the actions of others when times are good—when a company is strong and everyone is earning big bonuses. But you can also learn a lot from how people act when the ship is sinking. In fact, I've found that you can learn a lot more during the bad times, because that's when most people's true character emerges. It's like squeezing a tube of toothpaste. What's on the inside comes out when you apply enough pressure. When you apply enough pressure to a human, you'll see everything on the inside come out, and sometimes it won't be pretty.

When times are good, it takes a more discerning eye to see into someone's character. But if you look hard enough and observe their actions consistently over time, you'll be able to see an accurate picture of who they are. This is a process of learning, and it's important to do. Learning from other executives in the business world around you can prevent you from making grave mistakes. But ultimately, if you follow your own value system and a set of standards, the mistakes you make shouldn't impact you negatively. You'll still make mistakes now and then—all of us do—but they won't be damaging to your reputation or your career. If you watch carefully, you'll be able to learn from others in the business world around you.

•   •   •

The employees who worked at Enron before it collapsed have been out-spoken about the corporate culture there, and many have publicly stated that while they loved working there, there were also things they were uncomfortable with. That's a big red flag, and it's something worth paying attention to, because if your manager is making a questionable decision, or a colleague has blatantly violated an ethical policy and suffered no consequences, it's a sign that the highest levels of the company are uninterested in building a culture based on integrity. It's the day-to-day actions of others you can learn from, and not just the monumental ones. If you get this feeling about your company, it's time to move on. Life's too short to get caught up with one of the "cheater" companies.

Sherron Watkins, the former Enron accountant referred to in the media as the "Enron Whistle-blower," has described a culture of greed where there was continual pressure to network, impress people, and stay focused on the next big deal. There is a lot to be learned from the failure of others—in Enron's case, CEO Kenneth Lay and the rest of Enron's management team, who did little to cultivate a culture of integrity.

Watkins, who had worked in Enron's finance department under Chief Financial Officer Andrew Fastow, stumbled across complex partnerships backed by Enron stock. The deals were allegedly done to hedge Enron investments that were failing, but she could see that they were a ticking time bomb. After Enron CEO Jeffrey Skilling resigned abruptly in August of 2001, Watkins met privately with Kenneth Lay, the new CEO, about her concerns. She told him that the inconsistencies had to be uncovered. Watkins felt that if they would come clean, Enron would certainly be able to survive the impact it would have on the company, and they could restate their financial filings. But Kenneth Lay reportedly did nothing, and Enron didn't come clean. Enron management lacked transparency, and when the company went under, it negatively impacted thousands of people. The whole Enron experience is something we all can learn from. Business leaders can learn how not to be transparent by observing the way Enron executives handled their business, and every executive at any level should know how to detect behaviors and actions that aren't consistent with integrity. Small lapses in judgment have the power to destroy a career, and even a company, in the long run.

Early on in my own career I had the benefit of working with a lot of people who weren't terribly ethical. I look at it as a benefit, because it reinforced for me the message that honesty is the only way. This is something some people don't learn until late in their careers, and then sometimes it's too late. When I worked for Aaron Cushman and Associates early in my career, I was fortunate to be exposed to people whom the public held in high regard, and I learned from their behaviors and actions when they weren't in the public eye. I learned that a lot of them violated the first principle of transparency—tell the whole truth—and it was beneficial for me in helping to shape who I would become.

When Cushman's assigned me to work on the Paramount Pictures account, one of the most important accounts they had, one of my responsibilities was to make sure that the celebrities arrived at their television interviews on time. I met quite a few interesting characters. I learned a lot about integrity back then by watching and listening, and observing what *not* to do.

The Transparent Leader Is Willing to Be a Mentor

I've been fortunate to have some great mentors in my life. There are also colleagues and peers whom I admire for the way they do business—people like Reuben Mark, who isn't afraid to tell it like it is. People who have their priorities straight and egos in check are the ones I've found to be the most successful, and they're the kind of people who want to be good examples for others. They like it when they're asked about their business. They take the time to answer employee questions, and they've got their priorities straight.

Robert Pohlad, the chairman and CEO of PepsiAmericas, is one of those people with his priorities in the right place. Pohlad likes the challenge of building something the right way, and he does it to win. He considers his *employees* every bit as important as his shareholders. In my book, that's a good strategy. If your employees are happy, they'll work hard to build a strong company, and your shareholders will benefit. Pohlad runs a company with over $3 billion in revenues, but he schedules his business meetings around his son's soccer games because his children and his family are the most important thing in his life. He's a busy guy who enjoys the competitiveness of business, but he's been able to find balance in his life, which is something a lot of executives still can't seem to get right. And if you asked Bob about his job running a big company, he'd say that what he does isn't any better or worse than anything anyone else does—it's just a job.

Are you a transparent leader? I hope you'll think about it, because someone is sure to be watching, and you may not even know it. It may be the twenty-year-old in the mail room, or it may be the middle-aged guy with four kids who will pass on something he learns from you to his own son. Your mentorship might be accidental—through a brief moment of contact with someone, or over many years. Leadership comes with the responsibility of being a good mentor to others.

In my own career I've been fortunate to serve on boards with people like the Bob Pohlads of the world, but I've also learned a lot by watching people who aren't so good at being open leaders. Watching some people around me stumble, lie, and disrespect others gave me a lot of insight, and I learned that your integrity is something that you carry with you always, and it can be easily misplaced. If you don't have a transparent lifestyle you'll never be considered a high-integrity person, and though you might be remembered as a successful person, people will say other things about you that aren't so flattering. The old adage that it's not whether you win or lose but how you play the game is true—especially in today's business environment.

CHAPTER THREE

THE TRANSPARENT EMPLOYEE

I n the eighties, there was a bronze desk statue that was popular with some executives—it displayed three monkeys covering their eyes, mouth, and ears. The caption beneath the monkeys read: *See No Evil, Speak No Evil, Hear No Evil.*

It was a sign of the times, in an old corporate landscape when what you didn't hear or see didn't exist, and what you didn't say couldn't get you in trouble. But times have changed! Today it's all about seeing, saying, and hearing. Turn on any news channel and you'll see plenty of examples of executives who didn't see the things they should have, didn't say the things they should have, and didn't *hear* the things they should have. They learned the importance of seeing it all—even when it's not good news—but they learned it too late. By the time they figured out how essential it is to be transparent and cultivate transparent employees, their own employees were being investigated, their documents subpoenaed, and in some cases their companies shut down.

IN SEARCH OF CHARACTER

In an environment of true openness, it's the good of the entire organization that matters. The employees understand their own limits, and they value the talents and ideas other colleagues bring to the table. The corporate culture is open, ethical, and transparent as a whole, and every individual buys into the concept of making transparent decisions. This is transparency in action.

The best leaders I've encountered are the ones who know that there's no value in a yes-person. They don't look for people to boost their egos—they work on cultivating a good atmosphere of transparent employees, and they avoid the ones who seem like they'll see no evil, speak no evil, and hear no evil. They understand that the best employee is one with the fortitude to tell you what's really going on—for the good of the company.

But a major issue when it comes to attracting good employees is that a lot of people haven't been fortunate enough to have a solid mentor early on to teach them how to do business with integrity. The way they do business mirrors the attitudes and character of whoever mentored them in the corporate world, and if they were raised in the corporate excess of the eighties or the tech explosion of the nineties—where twenty-year-olds made millions on virtual companies valued at ten thousand times their worth—making ethical business decisions could be a very foreign concept for them.

Learning by Example

There are turning points in every person's career that shape the way they think and feel about where they're going and where they've been. When you reach the crossroads and have that moment of discovery, or "revelation," you learn something that you usually never forget, or you're exposed to someone who stays in your mind for a long time. I've had a lot of those moments in my career, and some caused me to take note of what kind of leader I *never* wanted to be.

One moment has always stuck in my mind as the perfect example of opaqueness, and what kind of leader not to be. It was on Halloween day, 1989, and I was sitting in a marketing presentation at Campbell Soup Company, next to Gordon McGovern, my boss and the president and CEO of Campbell Soup. I was the president of Campbell USA, and Gordon and I spent a lot of time together. We were sitting elbow to elbow in this meeting when the door opened and my assistant motioned me out. I left Gordon at the marketing meeting and was ushered into the office of Bob Vlasic (of the pickle clan), who was the nonexecutive chairman of Campbell at that time. I sat down and Bob read me a memo saying that Gordon McGovern had resigned and that I was to be an executive vice president of the company and acting co-CEO. I still scratch my head about that one. Here I was, just a minute before, sitting right next to him, but someone else had to tell me he was leaving the company! Talk about lack of transparency. I hadn't yet taken my first CEO job, but I knew that he wasn't the kind of CEO I wanted to be. And even before that moment when I learned he'd be leaving the company, I had insight into his character, because of the way he had treated me on several occasions. But those experiences helped me see the value of good ethics and understand that sometimes, people who don't think about the people aspect of running a company, and who don't make ethical decisions, rise to leadership positions anyway. Life isn't fair sometimes, and that's something we'll probably never figure out. But you have to do the best that you're capable of, you have to have high integrity, and you have to have faith that eventually those opaque people will get what they deserve.

Legislating Ethics

When Congress enacted the Sarbanes-Oxley Act of 2002, a lot of executives got a wake-up call. Sarbanes-Oxley, the package of corporate regulations designed to increase transparency and make executives more accountable, caused a lot of companies to shift their focus to the importance of integrity. Good business practices suddenly became the "in" thing.

The law caused executives and boards to increase the importance of corporate governance in their corporations, analyze the way numbers are reported and achieved, and scrutinize the way employees are developed. The enactment of Sarbanes-Oxley won't be the cure-all, because the effectiveness of how well values are ingrained in the business culture is ultimately determined by the actions and philosophy of a company's leader; but Sarbanes-Oxley is a start.

Sarbanes-Oxley is the biggest change to federal securities laws since the 1930s, and it's already altered the way corporations report their numbers now that directors, auditors, and executives are being held *accountable.* This is good news for companies whose leaders haven't yet embraced the concept of accountability, but there's also a very real cost associated with legislation like Sarbanes-Oxley, and it affects everyone—even the companies who already have governance and compliance issues under control.

When most people outside the small world of upper-level management in a public company hear about Sarbanes-Oxley, they think it applies only to CEOs and CFOs. It's true that they're the ones who, under the new rules, are personally responsible for certifying financial statements that must comply with the standards set by the Securities Exchange Act of 1934. However, the new legislation affects everyone in a company. Sarbanes-Oxley states that *anyone* involved in reporting a company's finances, including *any employee* who has concealed the truth about the financial health of a public company, is responsible. That means that if you're the leader of a public company, hiring transparent employees isn't an option—it's mandatory. If you're a leader in a position to hire (regardless of whether the company you work for is public or private), you'd better start searching for good *character* along with good credentials.

Legislation such as Sarbanes-Oxley can't build character in your employees, only a transparent leader can. But the law might just change how a company conducts business, even down to the way corporations dispose of documents. Now, any accountants for SEC-regulated companies must keep all audit or review work papers for five years after the fiscal period ends. And document retention can cover a lot of things— from emails to any other records that were created, sent, or received in connection with an audit, a review, or an investigation. The crime for disposing of them? A fine, or even a jail sentence.

Being a completely open company involves providing any information that an outside investor would want, and identifying (and explaining) intangible assets that have driven the rise or fall of specific numbers, or anything that could determine future results. It means hiring honest people, and making sure the ones you've already got know that character counts. But the true test of how transparent your employees will be is in the depth of the culture you work to build. If your employees are smart and savvy but lack good character, any business strategy you attempt to execute will be shorted and subject to failure.

THE IDEAL EMPLOYEE

Hiring people with good morals and values may seem like an obvious strategy, but let's face it—morals and values haven't been high on corporate America's list. They aren't things that are usually talked about in job interviews. Most hiring managers ask a candidate simple questions like: What was your previous position at XYZ Corporation?

Values are inherently personal, and we keep them close to our vest. Think about the last job interview you had, or the last person you interviewed. If you were on the receiving end of the questions, do you remember any that were centered on values? "So, George, give me an example of one lesson your mother taught you when you were growing up?" usually isn't on the interviewer's list of questions.

It's easy to see why people get confused about what the ideal employee really is. We've been conditioned to seek out impressive credentials, and we perk up at the sight of a competitor's company name on a résumé. If they were good enough for XYZ Corporation (insert your largest competitor's name here) we think, they'll be great here! Especially if they are still employed by XYZ and have valuable data to bring with them. But that's just a myth, and it's an obstacle that can trip you up—if that's all you're looking for. Some managers get so hung up on the status of the *company* a candidate came from that when they see the company name on the résumé, they're so impressed they can't see beyond mere corporate reputation. Some companies search exclusively for candidates from the top universities and don't mind admitting that they'd prefer a candidate from Harvard over any other. Prior work experience also carries a lot of weight, and if you're hiring someone from outside your company, he or she may seem attractive on paper, even if they're not a good candidate at all. But be warned: credentials aren't everything, and sometimes they can mask the true character of the person beneath them.

You don't have to search far for evidence of this. You can pick up any major newspaper and read about a highly successful and credentialed business leader who was convicted of some sort of fraud. It really doesn't matter where you went to school or what big title you had if you don't have ethics. Some people have a lot of success and are able to amass good credentials despite their underlying character flaws, and those are the people you have to watch out for. They look good on the outside, but on the inside they're not.

Why Do People Lie?

If you're a generally good person, it may not be natural to be on the lookout for people with poor ethics, or those who are used to taking shortcuts, but in this day and age you have to. Global businesses have developed a culture where cheating is natural, to the point where each and every year at least one executive makes the front page because it was learned that he or she lied on a résumé, falsified a reference, or made up a college degree. But it's hard to spot the cheaters, because they're normally quite good at cheating if they've gotten away with it in the past. And if a cheater has credentials, it's even harder. Jayson Blair, the now infamous *New York Times* reporter who admitted to making up hundreds of stories over the course of his career, and lying to his editors, was employed by one of the most prestigious newspapers in the world! Prior to that, Jayson's credentials included a job as the executive editor of his college newspaper at the University of Maryland. When he was twenty, Jayson attended a prestigious Poynter Institute seminar titled "Ethics and Leadership for College Editors and News Directors." It took a lot of years, and countless false story submissions for Jayson Blair's character to be revealed.

It's quite natural to place emphasis on credentials, but I always try to remind myself that even Ted Kaczynski (the Unabomber) was a Harvard graduate. If we could pinpoint why people with all the opportunity in the world end up on the wrong path, we'd be geniuses. The answer to why people lie and cheat will never be understood, because there are a multitude of reasons. But the solution—finding ethical people and building your world around ethics—is, fortunately, black and white. Ethics involves no gray area. You either have them or you don't. You can't be ethical sometimes and unethical at others if you're committed to transparency.

I was fortunate enough to have worked with the great advertising legend David Ogilvy, who had a unique perspective on the kind of people he wanted to hire. He said that he liked to hire people from the Midwest because they had a feel for how America thinks and operates. The people from the Midwest have midwestern values, and they would also understand consumers! I was at Campbell Soup at the time, and I had the opportunity to work with him frequently. Ogilvy knew that good character was more valuable than good credentials any day of the week.

Character over Credentials

Hiring people with ethics and a foundation of values is important, yet a lot of executives in hiring positions still get it wrong when they think about the character traits of the ideal employee. Despite the importance of ethics in a candidate, they still get hung up on credentials. Think about it. Most companies hire people for a specific job. Human resources posts a job description somewhere and the search is on. The goal becomes to match the job description to the candidate who fits, because he or she has the best credentials—so we're really not thinking about values-based traits at all.

It's a very normal and natural human process to look for skills. In corporate America, hard skills like college degrees, past positions, and things that can be found on a résumé take center stage, while soft skills like honesty, creativity, or an eye for serving the customer stay in the shadows.

That's the way it is, but I propose a change. Imagine where companies like Enron and WorldCom might be if they had focused on values. Thinking about prior work experience is perfectly normal, but hiring good *people* should be a prerequisite for the final job offer.

BUILDING A LEGENDARY CORPORATE CULTURE

HELP WANTED: Seeking nice, hard-working professional who knows right from wrong. Liars and loafers need not apply. Salary commensurate with ethical standards. Send resume with character recommendations and a letter from your mother to:

IDEAL CORPORATION. ATTN: HUMAN RESOURCES DEPT.

Anyone who has worked for me has probably heard me say, "If you can't be nice to others, you can't work for me." It sounds simple, but people skills are often ignored when strong credentials get in the way. If I had to create a help-wanted ad for the newspaper, I'd advertise to attract nice people with strong value systems. That's the secret to building a transparent culture. Hire and cultivate a pool of nice, ethical, transparent employees—with loads of talent.

Don't get me wrong, work experience is very valuable, and sometimes a good indicator of success. But we've seen a lot of instances where people have been moved to a position totally out of their core competency—to something completely new for them—and they've excelled.

The "people people" I described in Chapter 1 can relate well to individuals at all levels of the company, not only those who can help them get ahead. They're team players, and they strive for excellence because it comes naturally, and because they care about the customer experience from beginning to end. Because they're not solely motivated by the bonus that will come if they achieve their goals, they're not driven by greed. They're well-intentioned people who are motivated by other things, such as the desire to produce a superior product, to exceed the goals they've set for themselves, or to provide great service. Look for the people people first, if you want to take a step toward organizational transparency and a great company culture.

Step Number 1: Hire People with Values, as Well as Credentials

Transparency is exciting to watch when it takes hold in an organization! It's contagious, and it spreads fast, infecting individuals, then work groups, and then the company as a whole. Transparent leaders know this, and they recognize that the hiring and developing of employees is character-based, which means changing the standard way of thinking. Companies that want to be transparent have to focus on attracting the ideal *person* rather than the employee who best fits a written job description. Hiring too fast, in order to have a warm body in place, can be disastrous. I've fallen into that trap way too often!

At Dial, we try to hire good people first, and we work at continually teaching all employees about what doing business ethically can mean to them personally, and to the company as a whole. When I hire someone, I search for the caring individuals, and I also search for a creative spark by asking a lot of questions about the person's life and what achievement they're most proud of. I try to learn about their past achievements, and also about what they really think and feel about certain issues, and *how* they arrived at their achievements. Did they work hard, get lucky, grow at someone else's expense? Those are insights worth uncovering.

Then, too, when I hire someone, there are a few things I'm certain I want to avoid. I want to avoid the "yes" person, the employee who would rather flatter me than tell me the honest truth. I avoid people who simply "execute" in favor of those who "anticipate." People who are obsessed with execution are a dime a dozen, but an ethical, creative, think-ahead person with good character is an invaluable asset. To me, that's the ideal.

I'd like to think of this as an anti-business business book. It's more of an operating manual. The things we're talking about are good character, a solid work ethic, and a genuine desire to make good decisions. It's about integrity, and it shouldn't be so complex. But if this were a traditional business book and we needed to insert a formula for the transparent employee, it would look like this:

Good Character + Values-Based Decisions +
Quality Service Provider/People Person = Transparency

The formula demonstrates an ideal employee who has good character, makes values-based decisions, and strives to provide good service to people. The end result? A *genuinely* transparent employee. When you hire one good employee, you have a model for hiring and developing others, and if you work at it, a domino effect of transparency will be set in motion. At Dial, we call them "role models."

But you can't expect a simple formula to be the answer to your prayers when it comes to developing transparent employees. It's a full-time job that revolves around values, and the culture has to be built in the manner a house is—brick by brick.

In the first chapter we talked about the importance of defining core values. The concept is that if you work to develop great *people*, you'll have great *workers*. That's true, although the reverse is not. And that's where some people get tripped up.

It's possible to have high-performance employees who don't have good character, but eventually they'll fail. It might not be on your watch; in fact, they might perform very well for you—since everything in life and business is cyclical and we all go through stages. But eventually, if they do not possess good character, they'll fail. It's not unlike a star athlete who gets arrested for buying drugs and finds his career ruined because no team wants to draft him. His star power may have overshadowed his character flaws on the road to success. After all, every team wants a number-one draft pick, so it's easy to overlook the small things. But what do you do when your number-one draft pick fails you and you're left with a hole in your team? When the star athlete fails, falls, or leaves, his or her reputation is tarnished forever, despite past success. Substance and a strong character determine sustainability.

Step Number 2: Reward Good Values

In Chapter 1 we defined the three basic principles active in the construction of a transparent organization: tell the whole truth, build a values-based culture, and hire "people people." We know that it has to come from the top down, that each principle is a building block and that you can't have transparency without all of them. We know it's possible to encourage honest, creative employees who care about others, but is it realistic to think that you can establish values and get employees to adopt them? Honesty is intangible—you can't see it or prove it—and most people come to you with their values already established. Is it possible for a corporation to teach values? I think you can.

Here's how.

At Timberland, the thirty-year-old outdoor apparel company, values are promoted and even rewarded. The company offers a week's paid vacation to employees who work volunteering with local charities, and one day a year they close down operations so employees can participate in philanthropic projects. They build playgrounds, work with underprivileged kids, or serve food in homeless shelters, and this one day costs Timberland about $2 million. They do it year after year because they want to instill values and develop employees with a strong work ethic, and with a desire to serve others. This approach has paid off for Timberland, which receives thousands of résumés every year from people who cite the company's focus on values as a reason for wanting to work there.

I'm a firm believer in giving people a chance to live up to your expectations of them, but you have to be willing to set the standard, and you have to reward people when they reach it. If you're a leader, you can't have the attitude that you're above the small jobs or that you're above honesty. You have to be willing to get into the trenches and build, along with everyone else. Your employees will do what you do, and they won't do what you won't do. Live your personal values, and reward employees when they do, too.

Transparency, Transparency, Transparency

In the real estate industry there's a familiar saying about how to buy a home that's also a good investment, and that saying is: "Location, location, location." That's because a good realtor knows that location means everything, and that it can mean the difference between a great resale value and a poor one. There are other factors involved in buying a great piece of property, but if you choose a nice piece of property in the worst part of town, none of the other factors will matter when it comes to getting a return on your investment. Location is essential.

In the corporate world the equivalent is transparency, and the only way to make your organization transparent is to build an open business culture where employees make morally and ethically correct decisions. *Transparency is everything,* and hiring service-oriented employees who care about people will set a company apart, especially in industries flooded with competitors who turn out similar products. The company with the ethical employees and the good reputation will be the one consumers and prospective employees seek.

Step Number 3: Treat Service as an Asset

There are a lot of different facets to transparency, and the ability to provide good service is an important one. Good service is a reflection of values, which in turn is a reflection of good, honest, transparent leadership. Providing great service (whatever your business) is a big part of being transparent, but it's an asset most companies forgot about in the past decade.

Service used to be a hot corporate buzzword, and at one point every marketing brochure or ad campaign seemed to be peppered with promises of "excellent service." During the dot-com era service didn't really matter, because a lot of companies that didn't have any service, storefront, or employees were still being valued at thousands of times their worth! Service faded into the background, and corporate America shifted focus to achieving exponential returns. In the process, companies forgot about the importance of quality, customers, and values.

The transparent leader sees service as an asset, a point of competitive difference rather than a slogan in a business strategy. Service is so important that it should be valued and assessed in the way companies value their brand.

Why Is Service Integral to a Transparent Culture?

When I first got the notion to write a book, I wanted it to be about service. Service is something that's often overlooked, yet it's absolutely essential in the development of transparent employees. Teaching employees how to be good service providers is part of building a values-based culture, and if you can cultivate people who have a genuine desire to help others, those very same employees will tend to be open, honest, and able to see beyond themselves.

If an employee is "me-centered," the result is a take-no-prisoners style of decision making, where all decisions revolve around *survival.* But if an employee is genuinely focused on others, and cares about the customer or consumer experience, he or she will make decisions for the good of the team and will treat your company as if it's their own. They'll care about where the money goes, they'll care about how customers are treated, and they'll operate with the best intentions in mind.

For example, have you ever checked into a hotel and encountered a mumbling, incompetent desk clerk who won't make eye contact and insists there's not one room available until three o'clock in the afternoon? How would they know, you wonder, when they haven't even looked at the computer? Not *one* room? Then you're given a monotone explanation about how hotel policy dictates that check-in is at three o'clock. That's the policy, and they aren't willing to deviate from it. When that happens in an industry that's all about service, you know the entire stay will be bad even before you slide the key in the hotel room door.

When I experience bad service, whether it's from an airline, a restaurant, or a hotel, I start to question every aspect of the company I'm dealing with, starting with the philosophy of senior management. If the airline ticket agent treats me as if I'm doing her a favor by checking in, I wonder what kind of corporate culture the CEO has worked (or not) to develop, and then I wonder if the CEO even cares. The funny thing about bad service is that you always remember it.

Step Number 4: Stretch and Motivate Employees

You won't have a transparent business culture if all you've got is a bunch of bored employees who aren't passionate about what they do. You have to encourage change, stretch their potential to achieve more, and continuously motivate them—even if it means moving them out of one position and into another.

I had dinner one night at the home of an attorney friend who asked me what I thought the retirement age for a director on a board should be. I thought for a second and then told him that age really doesn't matter, but what does matter is the *number of years* the director serves. More than ten, I told him, is too much, because that's when you run the risk of sliding into the comfort zone. You lose your passion for the job, unless you're a very unique person who has lived to be in that position all of your life.

There are exceptions to every rule, but when he asked me the same question about CEOs, I put the limit at five. CEOs should start looking for a new job after five years or so, because any more than that and you start to run out of gas. After five years it gets harder to find fresh ways of looking at things, and you begin to perform on autopilot. That doesn't mean you can't be a CEO somewhere else, but it's my opinion that it might be time to juggle things a bit. It's the same way for employees in the same job too long. A transparent business culture is active, open, and invigorating. You can't let yourself get stagnant, and if you have employees, you can't let them stagnate, either. If an employee is left to stagnate in the same job he's had for the past twelve years just because it's something he's good at or comfortable in, boredom will set in, and it's hard to be effective and creative when you can do your job with your eyes closed.

Continually motivating employees requires a lot more than holding company pep rallies or annual sales meetings at fancy destinations. That's something every big company does. Motivating means intro-

ducing change sometimes, and stretching people on a daily basis by offering challenges to keep them fresh. I mix things up a lot in our own
company in an effort to keep our employees passionate about what
they do, and to keep their "shelf life" from expiring. I think it's important to keep them transparent, and I don't want to overlook the career
advancement of a person who runs a particular department just because she's so good at her job that she knows that department inside
and out and is "invaluable" in that position. It's easy to get comfortable with good employees who are really great at a certain job function, and to want to keep them there. But that's selfish, and it won't
help them grow.

I want to extend their reach, so their shelf life doesn't expire and
lead to boredom. I want to create a career path for them to keep the
fires burning and spark new passion and interest.

People are sometimes surprised here when they're asked to switch
jobs. They can say no if they want to, or they can jump in and accept
the challenge, but it's this type of openness that really stretches people.
At Dial, we did this with the head of our West Coast sales and the head
of supply-chain management, with the goal of challenging them to
grow. We were looking at succession and we had two very qualified
people. So we had to see who would rise to the challenge. By switching
roles, each person would have the opportunity to see how the other side
did it, and learn new things about the business. It shook things up a
bit, but they both learned a lot about themselves and what they
thought they wanted to do.

At Dial we work hard to keep employees happy, motivated, and
focused on the positive things involved in going to work everyday. If
someone in marketing decided they wanted a career in another department altogether, we'd try to make it happen; because part of keeping
the people you attract is creating opportunities for them to thrive and
learn. They'll be happier with where they are, and more likely to feel
part of the big picture.

Step Number 5: Provide Benefits
That Strengthen the Culture

Great employee benefits build morale and help strengthen a business environment by increasing employee comfort and confidence about being a part of the organization. Benefits reassure employees that you care.

Some companies work to encourage balance and values by offering basic benefits such as contributions to college tuitions, personal-development programs, fitness memberships, and other perks that add value to employees' lives. On-site fitness centers can be found at many corporations in America, and some have basketball courts, yoga classes, and even personal trainers. In south Texas there's no better place to work than USAA, the mega insurance company that has taken the concept of a balanced life to the extreme.

USAA has a very low employee turnover rate, and it's not hard to see why. If you're an employee at USAA, the everyday errands that take up time and add stress to your life are easier, because everything is on-site at the company's 286-acre San Antonio, Texas, campus. There's an on-site store where employees can buy toys for birthday gifts or even shop for Christmas, an on-site post office where the packages can be sent, and several restaurants where you can take home preprepared lasagna for dinner.

USAA's *culture* is legendary, because it offers employees unique benefits that other companies don't, like a carpool service for employees who don't want to drive to work; a flexible work schedule in which employees can choose from a traditional work week or even a three-day week schedule if they prefer; three fitness centers; health clinics; and acres of running trails, tennis courts, and softball fields. The corporate headquarters is arranged like a small town, with park benches, brick roads, and inviting sitting areas for employees, and there are ten cafeterias with varying food themes.

USAA provides insurance and financial services to military personnel and their families, and they've got a values-based culture that can be traced back to the company's founders—twenty-five former army officers who got together in 1922 to insure themselves after leaving the military. The company serves people who have served their country, and today that service-oriented mind-set still exists. Because they focused on values first, they established a culture that is strong eighty years later! By being good to its employees, USAA has cultivated a culture of employees who care, and when you have employees who care, you get employees who are honest and *transparent.*

Timberland and USAA are companies where values and teamwork are in action. The employees there feel good about themselves, their jobs, and their lives because the leaders of those companies understood the importance of building a values-based culture.

The Arrogant Corporate Culture: What's Transparency?

Some companies will never be transparent. These are the companies with leaders who believe they know it all and therefore they don't have to listen to anyone. The CEOs of these companies are just plain arrogant, and it's reflected in their workforce, too. They operate with a sense of entitlement, believe that they're the best in their field and always will be, and if they know what transparency is, they have no idea why it can benefit them. Call them ignorant, or call them arrogant, but most of the time they display a basic lack of good judgment that could eventually bring them down.

At one company I know of, there was a sign in the elevator on Friday announcing the beer and margarita party for employees in the company parking lot that afternoon. Makes you wonder what kind of business culture that CEO is trying to create, and how he could possibly overlook the potential for disaster, with a mix of employees, alcohol, and Friday-afternoon rush hour heading into the weekend. I also wonder what his customers think when they read the signs in the elevator on the way up to his office. I can't imagine that company would be able to achieve any sustained success with a corporate culture like that.

There's nothing wrong with a little fun—just ask Herb Kelleher of Southwest Airlines about using it to build a successful organization—but concessions that undermine a solid business culture lead to mediocrity, which makes it harder to do business with integrity. Why would an employee limit his drinking when entertaining a customer, if he's used to an environment that encourages partying it up with his manager and coworkers at the office? The small concessions that lead to a relaxed mind-set and business culture can filter through an organization from manager, to employee, to coworker, until your business units are infected. It's a domino effect, and the attitude becomes *just getting by with good enough,* rather than excellence, which causes employees to overlook small details that can derail the evolution of an entire organization. Are your standards high enough?

TRANSPARENCY SHOWS UP IN THE NUMBERS

Remember Reuben Mark, the CEO who called to tell me he was handed Dial's confidential competitive information? His company, Colgate, has a corporate code of conduct more than eighteen pages long that talks a lot about ethics, people, and trust. It's no accident that Colgate has had a success rate of 12.8 percent growth in earnings annually in the eighteen years he's been there.

The ancient concept known as karma—which is the idea that what you put out in the world comes back to you—may well be true when it comes to developing transparent employees. If you work to build a corporate culture with well intentioned employees who care about others, it will be felt by your customers; but if you create a culture of tyranny and fear, the customers will know it, and ultimately your business will suffer.

The idea of karma translated to the corporate world means that you have to be good to your employees in a lot of different ways and cultivate an environment where honesty and openness is encouraged, in order to get employees who will give all of that back. Good karma breeds good karma. Or, in other, perhaps simpler, terms: be transparent, and encourage your employees to be transparent, too. Your business will benefit from it. True transparency shows up in the bottom line.

PART TWO
THE PILLARS OF TRANSPARENCY

How did we get to today's toxic corporate environment? Have integrity and business ethics declined over the decades, or does it just seem that way? Part Two offers a brief history and evolution of integrity in business and establishes the pillars of transparency.

In Chapter 4, "The Evolution of Integrity," we look at the business leaders of some of America's largest companies to see how they succeeded, and where some of them failed.

Chapter 5, "Corporate Governance," gives insight into how to effectively govern a large organization and delves into the most common signs that a company is in trouble. If the executives at many fallen companies had paid attention to these red flags, they would be remembered in the history books as successes, not failures.

In Chapter 6, "The Communicative Leader," we talk about the biggest component of transparency: communication. Throughout the chapters in this section you'll learn about how integrity has evolved through the ages, how to keep it at the forefront of employees' minds, and how to see the red flags before it's too late.

CHAPTER FOUR

THE EVOLUTION OF INTEGRITY

> **OBITUARY**
>
> It is with great sadness that BUSINESS announces the death of INTEGRITY after a long and progressively debilitating illness. Integrity, born in the early days of civilized mankind, has often been known by such names as Honesty, Trust, and Decency. Integrity's passing went largely unnoticed as her absence became commonplace and her followers gave up hope. No monument will be erected to Integrity due to lack of popular support.

If you believe the headlines, integrity seems to have died. Everywhere you go the newspapers are filled with gloom and doom about dishonest CEOs, CFOs, executives arrested for fraud, and companies downed by corruption. Martha Stewart—the very definition of wholesome and home—accused of insider trading and convicted of obstruction of justice! Staunch and solid companies like Arthur Andersen, WorldCom, Rite Aid, and others, tarnished or ruined forever. Is integrity a thing of the past? To understand the answer, let's look at how integrity in business has evolved through the ages.

The word *integrity* comes from the Latin word *integritas,* which was commonly used in ancient Roman military tradition during the time of Julius Caesar. In the mornings, the Roman army would conduct inspections, during which a centurion would walk past each legionnaire to check his armor. Every soldier would take his right fist and strike his armor on the breastplate, which covered his heart, because the armor had to be the strongest over the heart in order to protect him from deadly sword thrusts and arrow strikes.

As a soldier struck his armor he would shout: *Integritas!* By that word he meant "completeness," "wholeness," and "entirety," and the inspecting centurion would listen for the distinct sound that well-kept armor made. Once he was satisfied that the armor was sound and that the soldier beneath it was protected, he would move on to the next man.

But by the time the fourth century rolled around, Roman society and its army had been affected by a great deal of social decline. Discipline in the army had become lax, and parade-ground drills had been abandoned. Soldiers stopped wearing their armor because it was heavy, and by the time the barbarian invasions occurred, breastplates and helmets were optional. The Roman army fought without protection against axes and arrows, and ultimately lost the fight. In other words, they lost their integrity. Sound familiar?

Integrity is a slippery slope. It's something I try to reinforce as much as possible with employees, not only in speeches and company presentations, but by doing the right thing. I learned early in my career that people tend to emulate who they work for, and it's important to be someone people know they can count on for the truth. But in today's world that trust is hard to earn.

Every time you turn on the television there's another story about an executive who succeeded in business by being unscrupulous. It almost makes you feel its okay. We've become immune. Scandal seems so prevalent in our generation because we live in an age where media coverage is overwhelming to the point where we're inundated with images and stories about corruption and deceit everyday. We watch executives in pinstripes being shackled and led by police from posh headquarter buildings, and we read about celebrity icons being investigated for securities violations. But unethical business practices are nothing new, and scandal has existed since the beginning of mankind.

In 1890, the Sherman Antitrust Act was implemented to regulate certain aspects of business. By 1914, the Federal Trade Commission had been created. Several executives were convicted of violating the antitrust act in the two decades that followed its birth, but it wasn't until the 1960s that anyone was actually sent to prison. This was because all business was seen as fair game, and executives who committed crime or bent the rules for monetary gain were viewed by society as cunning, strategic, and maybe even vile—but not criminal. There was crime in the corporate world, but white-collar criminals were seen mainly as shrewd executives.

The effects of scandal in American business were already being felt by 1915, when Harvard Business School began offering an elective class titled Social Factors in Business Enterprise. It was a course on business ethics and how social behaviors affect commerce. By 1916 Harvard had added a class on business policy and ethics that was part of the *required* curriculum. Even in the 1910s, business schools realized the need to educate students in ethics and integrity before they sent them into the business world, yet despite that early start, integrity has since been tested and compromised.

Just a few years after the Harvard course was introduced, the sports world experienced one of the most devastating scandals in its history when eight baseball players from the Chicago White Sox were accused of throwing the 1919 World Series against the Cincinnati Reds. The players on Charles Comiskey's White Sox team were among the best in baseball at the time, but Comiskey was a tyrant. Comiskey made a lot of notable contributions to the game of baseball, but his players were underpaid, and his harsh leadership tactics weakened morale. Even though he had two of baseball's biggest stars, outfielder "Shoeless" Joe Jackson and third baseman Buck Weaver, he paid each one only six thousand dollars a year, while less talented players on other teams were earning ten thousand dollars or more.

In 1917, when Comiskey's star pitcher, Eddie Cicotte, was on the verge of a thirty-win season, which would earn him a $10,000 bonus, Comiskey had him benched rather than risk having to come up with the extra cash. He was a terrible boss, but there was nothing the players could do because at that time a baseball player who refused to accept a contract was prohibited from playing on any other professional team.

Comiskey's closed leadership style backed players into a corner, causing a resentment that snowballed until they were vulnerable enough to succumb to a conspiracy that changed the game of baseball forever.

In the World Series of 1919, White Sox players intentionally made errors until Cincinnati won the final game 10–5. When word surfaced that they had conspired with gamblers to throw the Series, it was front-page news all over the country and eight well-known players were banned from baseball for life. It was a scandal larger than any other in its day, and as big as any we've seen in the headlines today.

That same year the most visible company in America was the Ford Motor Company. Henry Ford founded the company in 1903 with twelve shareholders and $100,000 in capital, and by 1924 he was producing two million cars, trucks, and tractors a year, perfecting the process of mass production and changing the way Americans lived. He was featured on the cover of *Fortune* magazine and lauded for his successes, but Ford also subscribed to Comiskey-like management techniques and became known as a dictator who refused to relinquish control of any part of the business. On top of that, Ford was widely criticized for his anti-Semitic opinions and writings, which regularly appeared in a newspaper he owned. Ultimately he paid the price for his harsh and closed leadership style. Ford's archrival, General Motors, posted higher profits than Ford every year in the sixty-year span from 1925 to 1985! Henry Ford and his Ford Motor Company are evidence that some CEOs became business legends simply because their name exuded power . . . despite the fact that their power contributed to bad business practices in their companies.

Even in the early 1900s, bad leadership didn't pay, and if today's business leaders had done their homework, they could have benefited by studying those who went before them. Granted, a hundred years ago autocrats weren't uncommon in business, because most of the men who owned companies had so much money and power that they called all the shots. There were no CEOs to speak of who were accountable to boards of directors, and by the 1970s, companies that were owned and controlled by just one person were a dying breed.

With the dawn of the nineties, one of America's more visible CEOs was Al Dunlap, later known as "Chainsaw Al." As the head of Scott

Paper, Dunlap boosted the company's stock price 225 percent by cutting 11,000 employees, slashing R&D and plant improvements, and all but eliminating corporate contributions to charity. When Dunlap sold the company to Kimberly-Clark he netted $100 million for just a year and a half's work, and in his best-selling autobiography, *Mean Business,* he boasted: "Most CEOs are ridiculously overpaid, but I deserved the $100 million. I'm a superstar in my field, much like Michael Jordan in basketball."

In 1996, when Dunlap went to Sunbeam Corporation, the company's stock price jumped 49 percent. He was revered by business leaders all over the world, and his tough management style was emulated and praised. But soon, the board of directors began investigating reports that much of Dunlap's turnaround success was based on little more than short-term accounting tricks, and he was eventually fined by the SEC. By that time, Sunbeam was trading at two cents per share. In the style of Henry Ford, Dunlap found out that being a bully and using control tactics on employees didn't pay in the long run and doesn't equate to good leadership.

After Dunlap, it seemed that America witnessed every kind of corporate scandal imaginable. At the start of the new millennium, executives at Enron, MCI WorldCom, and Arthur Andersen were accused of fraud and unethical business practices, and leaders of companies all across the nation were being scrutinized. In July 2002, the Securities and Exchange Commission filed charges against Adelphia Communications, the sixth-largest cable television provider in the United States, charging that Adelphia's founder, John J. Rigas, along with his three sons and other senior executives, conspired to commit fraud. Adelphia had excluded billions of dollars in liabilities from financial statements by hiding them on the books of off-balance-sheet affiliates and had reportedly falsified operating statements and inflated earnings.

The SEC learned that Adelphia executives inflated the key metrics used by Wall Street to evaluate cable companies by increasing their basic cable subscriber numbers, inaccurately reporting net income, and failing to disclose information such as the use of company money to build a $12.8 million golf club. Adelphia eventually filed for bankruptcy protection, adding to a long list of corporate scandals.

The list goes on. But this brief history lesson shows us that corporate misdeeds aren't going to go away. In America, we're getting closer to some sort of consistent thought process about what's considered acceptable, but we're still lacking a concrete model for all businesses to follow. There isn't a mandatory model for doing business and reporting information, and right now reporting varies from company to company, although Sarbanes-Oxley is getting us closer. Every industry measures things differently, and most *companies* measure things a little bit differently.

Internationally, the problems are just as complex. In Europe, executive compensation is being scrutinized. Even though American CEOs and executives usually earn far higher salaries, there's increasing pressure on European companies to tie executive compensation to performance.

In other nations bribery, deception, and dishonest executives have been a prevalent problem for years. In Argentina, for instance, fraud caused the start of massive reforms in the Argentine insurance industry, which has been plagued with corruption and bribery for decades. In that country, the structure of the insurance industry was set up so that a governmental body provided legally required reinsurance for all that had to be insured, and the structure caused a lot of opportunities for corruption because the governmental body accepted all reinsurance coverage, including bad risks. The result was excessive rates for customers, and bribes to governmental officials, which caused some foreign companies to capitalize on it by disguising their identities as investors in Argentina. There are a lot of other industries in other countries—including our own—that need reform. Transparency is lacking in many places all over the world.

INTEGRITY AS A STRATEGY

Integrity and its connection to successful leadership is a hot issue in the business world, and will continue to be now that corporations and executives have become aware of the dangers of deceptive business practices.

It's ironic that doing business with integrity has become the latest corporate trend, but sweeping reform will take place only when corporate America can regulate itself. This has to occur on an individual level, starting with the executives and leaders of companies, and the corporate world as a whole will need to join together to establish standards and best practices.

Once that happens, companies will have a model to follow, and executives will have a resource they can go to for answers on everything from how to disclose sales information, or executive compensation information, to how to report honestly and implement a values-based culture in the organizations they lead. Standards will be established for disclosure in different industries and departments, and the information disseminated will be much cleaner. That type of model for doing business transparently doesn't yet exist, but it's not so far away.

It's the leaders' responsibility to communicate values and how they connect to performance on the job. The best ones know that it's not just meeting the numbers but *the quality of the numbers and how you meet them that counts.* A government panel on ethics and more rules and regulations aren't the answer, and you can't regulate business across the board to create good behavior. Business needs to face up to its own problems.

Eliminating Company Politics

Conducting business with integrity is something that's always in the front of my mind, no matter what kind of negotiations or business deal I'm engaged in. I'm not perfect, and sometimes I make mistakes that I have to go back and undo. But if I'm in a meeting with an employee who has a complaint, or with an employee who wants to offer up a compliment, or if I'm negotiating an important business deal with a big customer—I always try to respond with integrity. That means no gray area, nothing but the whole truth, and fessing up when things aren't right on my end. It also means cutting through personal agendas to eliminate politics as much as possible.

With the need for speed in business transactions, and all of the other distractions that can pull employees away from the important things they have to do, internal politics is just another disrupting element. You have to overcome it in order to succeed in today's corporate climate, and that means continually inventing ways to keep integrity at the forefront in your employee's minds. Corporate politics are just a waste of time and energy. Things that draw you away from growth and into conversations and situations aren't productive. But every company has its share of politics—some so divisive that they tear at the fabric of the corporate personality.

At Dial, I do my part to eliminate company politics when it reaches my level, because if I can succeed at that, the message will flow downstream that corporate politics in general is a waste of time. Politics involves jockeying for position, a certain amount of deceit, working from a personal agenda versus the agenda of the team. This in direct opposition to the three principles of transparency we talk about in Chapter 1, and it goes against the steps required to build transparent, meaningful corporate culture.

I think a lot of CEOs like the politics that go on in their companies because it allows them a fly-on-the-wall view into different departments and managers, and they establish confidential sources who tell them what's going on. But that's counterproductive to true success and to the good of the company, because those confidants end up having a personal agenda that inevitably affects the stream of information going to the CEO.

When you let politics proliferate, you end up with employees who come in complaining about others, and then another employee comes in, and so on and so on, until you don't really know what the true facts are.

When there's a meeting that involves me in our company, I know that there are bound to be meetings before the meeting to prepare what will be said and how things will be presented. When an employee calls to schedule a meeting with me, it's not uncommon for me to get a call from *another* person in the company who has heard about it and wants to schedule an advance meeting to tell *his* or *her* side of the story. When employees calculate their moves like that it makes me angry, because it doesn't make for a transparent environment.

I've learned to deal with politics by maintaining objectivity until I've heard the whole story and can confront it head on. By confronting it right away, I find that the issues get resolved and the politics have no life.

Here's an example. An employee I'll call "Janice" came to my office with a lot of complaints about "Fred." I listened to Janice for a while and then I asked her to sit down in the chair in front of my desk while I dialed the employee she had come to me to complain about and asked him to join us! When Fred and Janice were face to face I said, "Okay, Janice, why don't you tell Fred exactly what you told me."

Needless to say, she was embarrassed, but she had no choice but to tell Fred what she had told me about him. They ironed it all out in about five minutes, and instead of letting the politics perpetuate until it turned into something bigger, we found a solution. It was a solution rooted in openness and integrity.

I believe that as long as there are two or more people in an office, there will always be office politics. You have to ask yourself how you can curb it and turn it into positive energy. The confrontational approach may not be for you, but there may be another solution you can find that's just as effective. Office politics, like gossip and rumors, is something that has the potential to bleed the teamwork out of your company. Personal agendas are not integrity-based, are counterproductive to a transparent culture, and are a waste of time.

Practicing What You Preach

Integrity is an important part of your business protocol as long as you're willing to be a leader who practices what you preach. If you don't, your employees won't respect you and they won't follow you.

When it comes to this rule, it's not just the big things that matter but the small ones, too. I'm a real believer that the early bird gets the worm, and I've been known to mention it a time or two in front of employees. I expect employees to get to work on time, not fifteen minutes or even five minutes after they're supposed to, and in my view it speaks to a lack of discipline when they don't. I'm an early riser, so I'm always in the office two hours before the normal starting time. But what do you think would happen if I decided to show up fifteen minutes after everyone else did? I'd be undermining our organization's goals and losing momentum as a leader. Employees would think that I wasn't capable of practicing what I preached.

In addition, I practice what I preach when I'm on the road for business. We've got employees who travel all of the time, and they stay in the hotels that our travel department has negotiated good prices with. I do the same; and even though many employees expect that I'd stay at the Ritz-Carlton, or some other expensive hotel, I stay at the cheaper ones. It's become fun to see if I can find the lowest rate in a decent neighborhood, and when we travel to New York City to visit the financial community, we pay just $189 a night! That's hard to do in Manhattan.

Good leaders work hard to set an example that shows that they mean what they say and say what they mean. Their employees can see firsthand that the executives at even the highest levels of the company truly desire to be honest and transparent, and that they have the best intentions in mind.

THE JOURNEY TO TRANSPARENCY

Like a lot of CEOs, I'm often asked to speak at college commencement ceremonies. In 2002 I was asked to address the graduating class of the University of Phoenix. There was an unusually large amount of press about corrupt CEOs at that time, and the newspapers overflowed with stories of corporate fraud. Students were gravitating away from the business world in record numbers, and the perception of corporate business leaders was at an all-time low. I knew that there was a chance they'd regard me as just another untrustworthy CEO because they didn't know me—and I also knew that because of their youth, they didn't have the benefit of witnessing the evolution of integrity, unless it was something they had studied. Integrity has ebbed and flowed. It's often been compromised, but it's always been important, and I wanted to let them know how important it would be to their success. I wrote them a letter that they could keep close at hand.

Letter to the Graduates

April 14, 2002
To the Graduates,

I was once where you are now. I started a journey many years ago and was fortunate enough to find my way to the pinnacle of my field. I hope all of you are similarly fortunate. But rather than just wishing you luck, I'd like to leave you with some tips that may help you navigate the complex world of business.

While each of you must find your own path to success, there are several things to keep in mind that will help you on your way. First, you need a map for your journey. By now you should know where you want to go and what direction to take to get there. Indeed, today you have completed an important step toward that destination.

Second, you need the skills and tools to apply your intelligence to the obstacles that stand between you and your goal. Again, the completion of your education here is an important step forward. But the learning does not stop today. In many ways, it only begins. Third, you need to have both drive and patience. This is no contradiction but a reflection of reality. Enduring success does not happen quickly and it never happens for those who quit at the first setback.

Fourth, you need the help of others. Recognize that the most valuable assets you will ever have are smart employees, loyal colleagues, wise mentors, devoted friends, and a loving family. And fifth, you'll never get anywhere worthwhile without a moral compass to guide your way. Regardless of what the media says, greed and avarice have no place in business and will only lead you to failure. You will face decisions of right vs. wrong and even more difficult ones of right vs. right. Only with a firm ethical keel will you be able to make the right choices.

Remember that toward the end of your journey there will be a time when you find yourself alone looking in a mirror. After all the work, the experiences, the setbacks, and the triumphs it will come down to one thing. When you look at yourself in that mirror—do you like what you see? If you've acted with integrity, that's all that matters. If you haven't, then nothing else does. Remember that and you're already a success.

Sincerely,
Herbert M. Baum

In my letter I didn't talk about turnarounds, charisma, celebrity, or becoming the next Donald Trump. I didn't write about strategy, return on investment, or how to increase the stock price. I wrote about integrity, because after all is said and done, your integrity will be remembered, regardless of what you achieve.

The history books are filled with stories about the achievements of people like Bill Clinton, Charles Comiskey, and Henry Ford, and right there among the accomplishments are the way they conducted their lives—for everyone, including their children and grandchildren, to read. How do you want to be remembered?

Some may point to the men and women who have succeeded in business without being ethical to illustrate that success can come without honesty. But that's a risky way to go, because eventually it catches up with you. So even if you don't believe in doing the right thing simply on the basis of good ethics, it's worthwhile to do the right thing to keep yourself, or your colleagues, out of jail. You can be a celebrated CEO, or an executive who prefers to stay out of the limelight, but regardless of your leadership style, do it transparently.

CHAPTER FIVE

CORPORATE GOVERNANCE

I n 2003, the Progressive Corporation, the leading Internet seller of automobile insurance, decided to emphasize their focus on transparency, by featuring a full two-page photographic spread of a naked man in their annual report. The title of the ad was "Bare All."

It was a bold move that highlighted Progressive's desire to be a forward-thinking, transparent company, and it got them noticed! They had made a commitment to transparency, and part of that plan included releasing financial information on a monthly basis, versus quarterly like everyone else, and letting the world know that they intended to be a different kind of company. It was a refreshing approach, and one that set the company apart from their competitors.

That type of straightforwardness is rare in most companies, but it's become a lot more common these days, and it's essential if you're faced with the challenge of turning a company around. You have to be honest with employees, but also with the general public, and you have to address corporate governance issues head on.

WHAT IS GOOD GOVERNANCE?

Governance may be defined as the process by which decisions are made, and the definition of good governance in a corporation involves making decisions that benefit your shareholders and establishing business processes that will build trust and shareholder confidence.

Good governance begins with transparency. Greater transparency is the foundation that will give shareholders a clear understanding of your company, which will lead to increased shareholder confidence and build value. Executives in corporations and industries across the globe are striving to understand the definition of good corporate governance in an effort to establish the best practices across the board, but by now most experts and transparent executives agree that for good corporate governance, the best practices must include the following four components:

- communication
- compliance
- knowledge
- transparency

Communication is a vital part of transparency and good governance. Investors now seek critical company information via the corporate website, where they expect to find current press releases and information on the company, a current code of conduct, and a cultural contract (if there is one), among other things. A company with good governance practices posts all relevant information about itself and its cultural and financial information on its website in plain English. It's not hidden in reams of data on the investor relations page. It's easy to locate and simple to understand. The kind of information companies should post includes governance guidelines, and how the company implements them. Communication is a critical component of corporate transparency.

Compliance involves simply meeting all of the requirements necessary to comply with regulations, and then linking the communications aspect to it by making that information available to everyone. Compliance information should be posted on the internal website (or employee intranet) and also on the general corporate website for analysts, shareholders, and the general public.

Comprehensive information is another component of good corporate governance because it involves understanding the effect the competition can have on your business. Having intellectual capital in place is important in order to analyze and strategize a solid action plan for building your business. A good flow of accurate information will help the better companies maintain shareholder value by understanding market conditions and being able to anticipate how they will impact the company long term. Using knowledge effectively involves internal analysis of your competitors and anticipating what their future business strategies might be.

The last component to a good corporate governance process is transparency. Transparency builds trust, fosters good dialogue and communication, and encourages honest reporting and open and ethical business practices. You can't implement an effective corporate governance plan without it.

IMPLEMENTING EFFECTIVE GOVERNANCE

Good corporate governance is transparent. It means giving shareowners what they expect; it includes avoiding litigation and anything else that drains capital, and building the company's strength and reputation. When corporate governance is implemented correctly, the greater accountability involved will lead to transparency and ultimately business success.

Where Do We Start?

CEOs and their corporate-governance people have a lot more resources to draw from today than in the past, what with the recent proliferation of roundtables and seminars on corporate governance and surveys and other information that didn't exist before. The Association of Top CEOs is one organization that is helping leaders remain transparent through their on-campus "Ethics Institute" at the Darden Graduate School of Business Administration at the University of Virginia, in Charlottesville.

The Darden School is already a great resource for business students

(I spoke to an MBA student group there and found them to be first-rate), but the ethics curriculum will also support business leaders who need resources on implementing good governance plans and programs that will help them establish rules for doing business ethically. Organizations like that will continue to pop up in the next decade, and will be great resources to help executives tackle the complex issues surrounding corporate ethics.

Despite all of these new resources, there are still some people who have a hard time believing that a company can instill ethics and move grown employees to comply with good behavior standards. After all, how do you teach people to follow one set of rules after they've spent a lifetime without them?

B. Espen Eckbo, the founding director of corporate governance at Dartmouth College, said in a recent article in *Business Week* magazine, "You cannot teach ethics to a 55-year-old CEO with a big ego."

If Eckbo is right, we've got a tough battle on our hands, because transparency comes from the top. If the CEO doesn't have strong ethical values, no one else can be expected to either. The old saying that "you can lead a horse to water but you can't make him drink" might be half true. You can lead a CEO with a big ego to water, and if he gets dunked maybe he'll understand that his job is at stake. But it shouldn't have to come to that. Boards of directors and CEOs have to want to instill strong ethical practices into their companies. Those that resist will have a tough time with sustained success.

Legislating Corporate Governance

But the legislation that has now developed as a result of a few bad apples means that today's leaders cannot ignore corporate governance issues, and they must prepare themselves for the increasing costs of compliance to legislation designed to enforce governance. Sarbanes-Oxley, for example, generates very real costs for public companies in the area of administration and accounting, to the tune of as much as millions of dollars for a single company. I had been tempted to include the cost of compliance with Sarbanes-Oxley in the Dial Corporation's annual report (prior to our acquisition by Henkel KGaA) so our share-holders will understand how much government legislation affects the cost of doing business. But Sarbanes-Oxley isn't something that's going to go away, and companies will have to plan its costs each year.

Some people believe that the technology costs associated with the law will be even larger than what it cost companies to get systems ready for Y2K, because Y2K was a one-time thing. Sarbanes-Oxley is ongoing, and there are costs associated with this new corporate-governance legislation that still haven't been fully calculated. This is the cost of corporate shenanigans, and corporate America brought it on itself.

Sarbanes-Oxley created changes that involve the allowable time to file quarterly reports, which will fall from 45 days to 35 days by 2005. Annual reports will have to be filed within 60 days of the close of the year, rather than the 75 allowed today, and disclosure of "material events" and insider trades must be filed within two days of an occurrence. All of these new rules may impact the reliability of the old systems that some companies have in place and could cause them to have to make costly changes to implement new computer programs and documentation to comply. At Dial we're up to date, but what about the companies that aren't? They'll have to figure out exactly what they need to do to get on the compliance bandwagon right away. Some companies will have to install new systems to speed up the reporting process and to make sure they can meet the reporting deadlines.

Another cost associated with legislation such as Sarbanes-Oxley could involve systems security, because the integrity of a corporation's data has to be pure and current. The problem is that anytime you have humans manually entering information into computers or order-processing systems, you've got the potential for error, so leaders of companies will have to work to make sure their organizations informa-tion technology departments are on top of all of the technical issues that affect compliance. These are things that will be scrutinized by leaders of companies for decades to come, as they race to keep up with the rising costs associated with corporate-governance legislation and the time it will take to comply.

The Cost of Good Governance

Throughout my career I've been lucky to work with companies whose brands are household names—Campbell Soup, Dial Soap, Quaker State Motor Oil—but a lot of them have been in turmoil, and turning them around has been a challenge. In every turnaround situation I've been involved in there have been similar issues to tackle, like what it will take to reduce costs and pay down debt, and how to build or rebuild brand strengths and consumer confidence in product quality. But the biggest issue is always the corporate culture. You have to know how well values and integrity are understood and appreciated, and you have to have specific corporate-governance measures in place to protect the culture you hope to build.

Good governance is a necessity in building a strong corporate culture, and bad governance can be the death of a culture. When I was at Campbell Soup, we had a strong set of values that had been established by Jack Dorrance, the son of the founder. I learned from him the importance of always doing the right thing, and I learned that product quality is paramount. I also learned that the reputation of the company is critical to maintaining corporate strength. Campbell Soup was and is a company with soul.

One of the companies I was involved in turning around was Quaker State Motor Oil, which, before its acquisition by Pennzoil, and ultimately by Shell Oil, was a $600 million company that provided motor oil, oil and gas production, automotive warranty insurance, and truck lighting. The company had a rich history, starting in 1859 as a small marketing company that produced Pennsylvania crude oil products to lubricate steam engines, machinery, and wagons. When the nation entered the mechanical age, oil became the lifeblood of industry and transportation and Quaker State products were a hit with consumers. Quaker State had been a great company, and was actually the number-one brand of motor oil throughout the 1960s. But then it lost its way. By the time I joined Quaker State as chairman and chief executive officer in mid-1993, Quaker State had hit the skids, and I was charged with turning the company around. It had slipped to the number-three brand position and was still heading south.

There were things to clean up at Quaker State, and at the Dial Corporation, too. Problems at companies can be the result of bad management, a poorly executed strategy, or shabby corporate governance, but at Quaker State it was a lot of different things combined. It was my responsibility to establish best practices and clean up any messes that were causing the company and its shares to slide.

One issue we had to clean up at Quaker State involved the Heritage Insurance division, which specialized in extended automobile warranties. The division had been sued by an agent who had lost his agent status. He was, to make a long story short, terminated by Heritage. He sued Heritage and also Quaker State in the state of California, so Quaker State hired a California lawyer to represent its side of the case. Shortly after I joined the company and sat down with our general counsel to sort things out, he estimated the lawsuit could cost Quaker State a maximum of $50,000 in penalties. Fifty thousand dollars wasn't a big number for a lawsuit, and since I had appeared on the scene late in the game I trusted the judgment of the people familiar with the lawsuit. What a mistake. Just two weeks after I arrived at the company, the California jury came in with a penalty verdict of $22 million. Twenty-two million! That's $21,950,000 more than our attorneys had estimated. You can imagine my shock.

Remember, governance is the process by which decisions are made. *Good governance* is about making decisions that benefit your shareholders. Eventually Quaker State (Heritage) settled at $9 million, a decision we made with the best interests of the shareowners in mind. We settled because we had to begin paying interest immediately on the full judgment amount—in this case, $22 million—from the day the judgment was rendered. That would have been quite costly. So we settled for just under half that amount, but still a lot more than $50,000. I learned a lot from that experience, and not all of it was good. For one, I learned that we live in the most litigious society anywhere in the world. California courts are like the Wild West! I learned that you might as well settle, even if you think you'll be treated fairly going to trial because when it comes to a jury and a corporation, the jury is often biased toward the "little guy" against the big corporation—even if the corporation is right. But I also learned firsthand how good governance sometimes involves making difficult and costly decisions because it will benefit the shareholder in the long run.

That experience affected my decision when, later on, Quaker State was sued for price fixing (along with a lot of other Pennsylvania oil companies) based on alleged violations that occurred before I joined the company. I found myself cleaning up another mess, even though it was an absurd claim. This time Quaker State settled early for about 25 percent of what the other oil company defendants were forced to pay after they went to court. I learned that if you really want to make things happen quickly, sometimes you just have to pick your battles and decide what's best for your company, your employees, and your shareholders. In the society we live in, you'll be safer if you settle. Sad . . . but true.

TOOLS TO ENFORCE GOVERNANCE

At Quaker State we implemented controls and established processes for good corporate governance way ahead of our time. I personally certified the financial statements, along with the CFO, and we did a lot of the things Sarbanes-Oxley calls for today.

The corporate-governance message has to filter down to the employees below the upper- and middle-level management teams or you might as well not think about it at all. The entire company has to know what it is, and why it's important. Communicating the message of good governance means setting basic rules to evaluate things such as a board's role in the success of the company, with issues like executive compensation, acquisitions, and succession.

Good governance is a long-term process, and for some companies it may even require hiring corporate-governance managers to enforce it, or implementing specific risk-management solutions for detecting fraud, such as toll-free hotlines. There are a lot of different tools a company can utilize.

Effective Corporate Boards

By now we all know that a culture based on values has to come from the CEO, but the role of the board is just as important. There was a time when board members might not have been so involved in the direction of the company, but today's boards need to be different.

Since 2001, massive corporate-governance changes have swept through corporate boardrooms, affecting the way companies report earnings, pay executives, and manage board expectations. The board of today has to give wise counsel, and in some ways the board has to participate in the strategic direction of the company. I'm not talking about values; I'm talking about offering advice on things such as the company's posture on acquisition candidates, participation in discussions on vision and strategy development, and asking tough questions about business performance. A good board does this by understanding the business, getting to know key executives, and offering sound financial oversight.

General Electric's board played a key role in setting a corporate-governance precedent when it stepped forward as a compensation pioneer by eliminating stock options as a form of compensation for its chairman, Jeffrey Immelt.

GE's board decided to pay shares based on performance targets, as part of an effort to overhaul the compensation program and focus on performance. It was a precedent-setting move and is likely to move other companies to do the same, and it was designed to use cash flow as the barometer instead of earnings.

Immelt wrote in his letter to stakeholders in GE's 2003 annual report: "Working with the board, we established a few principles about my pay. Namely, it should be transparent, performance-based and aligned with investors. To reinforce this alignment, I will no longer receive stock options or restricted stock. Instead, I will receive 'performance share units.' "

Compensation programs like that offer shareholders an honest view of how a company is doing, because cash flow can't be manipulated like earnings can. Cash is king. You either have it or you don't. A strong corporate board demands a transparent company.

Reporting and Compensation

In 2001, E-trade's CEO, Christos Cotsakos, resigned over a controversy concerning an $80 million pay package he received when the company's shares were spiraling downward. The new CEO, Mitchell Caplan, was credited with turning the troubled company around, and he started by focusing on corporate governance and implementing strategies to transform E-trade's image. The new E-trade set out to exceed the standards set by Sarbanes-Oxley by redesigning its board to have all outside directors. This meant that company-affiliated directors had to leave the board, and E-trade would have to find new ones—an increasingly popular strategy at corporations that had been confronted by some sort of scandal. But replacing directors is just one small step toward regaining the confidence of shareholders. Sometimes the leader has to take a hard look in the mirror and address how he or she is compensated.

Compensation is a big hot button for me. I get uncomfortable whenever I feel like a CEO is taking a lot of money at the expense of the company, the employees, and its shareholders. A lot of CEOs are paid far too much. But it's not just about CEOs. Professional athletes are also overcompensated. They provide entertainment (and so do some CEOs at times!), but athletes earn far more money—sometimes tens of millions—than a teacher, or even a surgeon, who saves lives. Another overcompensated group are lawyers, specifically class-action attorneys and plaintiffs' lawyers who claim to be Robin Hoods for the mistreated. Sometimes they actually do represent people who need representation, but a lot of times they're not doing anything beneficial, and they end up taking a huge cut of the settlement for themselves. My wife, unbeknownst to me, sent in a form to participate in a class-action lawsuit as a plaintiff. They had her fill out several forms—proofs of purchase and so on—and she finally received a settlement payment of . . . fifty-two cents! How much do you think the attorneys made? The way people are compensated in our society, and in corporations specifically, is one of the major governance issues in need of reform.

When I arrived at Dial, the board of directors wanted to compensate me with a bonus for my first partial year (five months). I declined because the performance for the full year wasn't good. Why should I be compensated for walking through the front door? I hadn't done anything yet, and there weren't any earth-shattering improvements to talk about. So I met with the management team, talked to our key customers, reviewed the numbers, and drafted a strategy to turn the company around. We presented the strategy to our shareholders and employees. We went public in the media with the challenges we faced, both financially and organizationally, in just two months!

Good Succession Planning

I don't think it's an accident that the word *success* is embedded in the word *succession.* Investors buy the future of a company, not necessarily the company it is today, and that's what owning shares is all about. You're buying based on a future higher price per share, and future earnings. That's why succession at the CEO level is an important part of corporate governance. Yet, the shareholders know that the company is more than just the CEO, because he or she is just one person. That is why some shareholders and analysts like to know several members of your management team just as well as they know your financial statements.

Investors are really evaluating investments in future earnings streams, so it's natural that they'd be interested in current management, and also who's available to succeed them. Good succession planning is a process that reveals the strong candidates, but also the people who aren't performing as well as they should. It points out a company's strengths and weaknesses.

I've seen people sometimes leave as a result of the succession-planning process after we put them in positions to stretch their capabilities, to determine how valuable they'd be in a future, more challenging, role. When you discover people who aren't performing and aren't capable of achieving higher standards, you learn that they can block more talented people from thriving. This is something we take seriously at our company because it's people, not just the CEO, who drive our success.

At Dial we do succession planning right down to the regional sales manager level. When you go to that level you find yourself looking at department managers and section heads, at people all across the ranks. This gives everyone an equal opportunity to really rise up through the company.

In a good succession plan, the incumbents at mid-levels should be held responsible for identifying their own replacements. The leader should communicate the importance of succession and build it into performance reviews. There have been too many times when I've had to tell someone that they didn't get a job they were qualified for because they didn't have a replacement. True succession is more than just going through the motions to get and retain great people. It's the only way to build a company, and it's a prime responsibility of the board to urge management to have a strong, actionable plan in place.

At Dial, two members of the board were appointed, along with me, to form a management-succession committee. The committee has worked to become familiar with key members of my staff and determine if there are potential internal CEO successors so they can give the remaining board members counsel on the candidates. The initial emphasis was on having the committee, representing the board, become familiar with these people in a social situation. It's a comprehensive process, but the board makes the final decision. I'm a member of the committee, but CEO succession isn't dominated by my opinion, although that was a common practice in many companies in the past.

In previous decades, some companies had nonexistent corporate-governance standards and it wasn't uncommon for a CEO to nominate a friend or family member. The board, which in some cases consisted of the original CEO's friends or family members, complied, and it was an interwoven system where everyone was closely connected. The process we've got at Dial is totally open, and if the committee isn't confident that the internal candidates can be ready for my departure, an external search will begin.

A strong company addresses succession at a lot of different levels. Succession is a facet of corporate governance that strengthens the entire organization and makes it stronger and more attractive to investors. Good succession planning is a sign of good governance, because it sends the message that leadership is a serious subject.

Governance Hotlines

Corporate governance is ineffective if employees refuse to buy into the idea and if they ignore it when a colleague does something unethical. Your corporate culture has to be based on real, meaningful values for corporate governance to be effective.

Prior to Enron, it was common for employees to suffer in silence for fear of retribution, and in a lot of companies the attitude seemed to be that if the boss was breaking the rules, there was no way to report it without going through the boss first. But the rules have changed, and in the environment we're in now transparent employees know that it's important to speak up.

Some companies are taking measures to protect employee privacy by using hotlines as an anonymous way for employees to provide feedback. This is something we've done at Dial, and if an employee calls our hotline he or she knows the call will be anonymous. No fear and no retribution. That's the deliberate corporate culture we've worked to create.

If an employee called the hotline to report an accounting violation, for instance, the concern would go to the head of the board of director's Audit Committee, and then it would be presented to the full board. It would bypass me, and I'd never know the name of the person who placed the call.

Overall, a governance hotline gives employees anonymous ways to call in any suspicion of wrongdoing, and we get all kinds of calls—not just complaints or negative feedback. It's a valuable way of understanding the needs of employees, because when an employee calls our hotline, they know there won't be any repercussions because we've promoted a culture of openness. Some people criticize such an open reporting system because it encourages whistle-blowers; but as a CEO, I'd like to know if there's a whistle that needs to be blown! I encourage whistle-blowers, but I also hope that we've created a strong ethical culture where it won't ever be necessary.

BUILDING GOOD GOVERNANCE THROUGH EMPLOYEES

A lot of leaders forget that their people are more than just important—they can make or break you. People play a huge role in setting the corporate culture, bringing a sense of urgency to the corporation, and governing the actions of other employees in their workgroup. Good people help breed good habits in each other, and they do it because they have the interests of the entire employee group in mind. That doesn't mean you have to turn your employees into tattletales; but it does mean that good governance should exist at all levels of the company.

First you have to develop a categorical imperative for business practices, which translates to the greatest good for the greatest number, and then you have to educate your employees on how to spot ethics violations if and when they occur, and set the right tone for policing those that can bring negativity into your culture.

Education is a big part of building a corporate culture, because how can you expect employees to know what your vision is as a company if you don't sit them down and present it logically, in a way that makes sense?

I've seen companies invest a lot of money in employee training programs, and in consultants, sponsored by the company's human-resources group, who preach "the ideal"—with no ultimate beneficial impact. What a waste of money! If you're going to invest the time and money to train your employees, you should be committed to understanding what motivates them (and what de-motivates them) and the CEO should not only be involved in designing the training plan, he or she should also *take* the training with the employees. It's time well spent.

Good Governance Includes Protecting Assets

At Dial we've taken some unique steps to ensure that our people assets are not only protected but cherished. One way we do this is by enforcing a policy that prevents anyone at Dial from being fired (heaven forbid!) unless it's first discussed with and approved by the CEO. That's me. The way it usually works is that the head of human resources will come to my office and make a case for why the employee isn't working out, and I'll ask questions like why doesn't the manager feel that he or she can develop the employee to become part of the team. I don't do it to micromanage; I do it to make sure we're protecting our greatest asset. It makes our managers think twice about pulling the trigger, and it incentivizes them to work harder at developing their people. I feel personally responsible for making sure our employees are treated fairly. I try to do everything to retain the talent we already have, and I consider it a process that protects the shareowners' best interests— so that our human capital isn't wasted. That's essential, and it's a part of good leadership, and good governance.

Despite all of that, sometimes we're faced with an ethical or performance issue that forces us to let someone go, and in that situation it's probably the best possible solution for the individual, too. You shouldn't keep someone you know can't succeed in your corporate culture, because you're doing them a disservice when you do. They might have a better chance of succeeding somewhere else.

This also applies to borderline employees. A borderline employee is one who just doesn't perform well within your organization for one reason or another. Maybe they're unhappy with your corporate culture, maybe they don't fit well within their workgroup, or maybe they just don't like the work they do. Before you let someone go you need to let them know where they've fallen short and why they can't stay, and then let them move on with dignity as quickly as possible. When they exit your company they should feel like they were treated fairly, and leave with their head held high. Hopefully they'll be a good fit somewhere else, or maybe they'll come back to you one day, or even send another potential employee your way. If you're a leader, you have to understand that people have feelings, and most people have personal pride. Take the time to understand it. It's a good business practice, and it's positive, transparent leadership.

If there were a best-practices method for achieving good governance it would be to communicate all the information you can about your company, its structure, its performance, financials, and business strategy in plain English to the appropriate audiences, while making sure that your employees are all doing the same. But it doesn't stop there. You also have to take it a step further and anticipate all of the things that you think might be lingering in the minds of people outside your company who need to know. If you anticipate possible questions before they're asked, and explain the answers clearly, you'll be viewed as up front and open. If you can explain why executives are compensated a certain way, for instance, instead of simply listing the compensation figures, investors will understand the rationale behind the company's actions.

This ability to anticipate is among the best skills anyone can have, and it's a big part of successful corporate governance. When you anticipate, you're thinking ahead, listening to your constituencies, and disclosing—before you're asked—information they'd find valuable. I believe the ability to anticipate is one of the most important traits of success, and I look for it when I interview people for key positions. I have a stamp in my desk that I often use when I'm returning memos to my staff. It says ANTICIPATE, and it's a great reminder of what I expect from them.

Anticipation simply means seeking to understand a situation *before* it becomes an issue. It helps you stay ahead of the game, and it includes identifying potential changes in the marketplace, in your industry, and in consumer shopping habits. Anticipation means staying ahead of the game—and doing it before your competitors.

GOVERNANCE AND THE INVESTIGATIVE CONSUMER

David Ogilvy, the late advertising great, once said: "Never underestimate the consumer. She is your wife."

Today's consumer is smarter than ever. The consumer today is an investigator, armed with information about products, services, and the reputation of the corporations he or she buys from. This new breed of consumer uses the Internet as a weapon, does his or her homework, and expects honesty.

There is also a growing trend of consumer advocacy. There are watchdog groups in nearly every industry that will analyze your product quality, your business performance, and expect clear and honest answers, and high standards. There are people who make it their full-time job to analyze your value, products, performance, customer service, and the means by which you manufacture and distribute.

You don't have to look any farther than the medical profession for an example of how consumers have transformed from acceptors of information to investigators. Traditionally, doctors were viewed as experts, and what they said about your health was the final word. If a doctor told you your child had allergies, you'd give your child the medicine the doctor prescribed. But society has changed, and the expectations of the patient have changed along with it. Now doctors meet with a lot more skepticism, and patients come into their offices armed with questions about treatments and procedures. The Internet has fueled this information transparency in large part by offering patients instant access to case studies, research reports, and published data on a variety of diseases, medications, and treatments, making the medical profession—and every other industry—an open book. Before meeting with a doctor, a patient is likely to search the Internet for the doctor's lawsuit history, credentials, and background. The investigative consumer is your company's chief corporate-governance official. With people looking into every corner of your company, and so much information readily available, governance and transparency is there, whether you like it or not.

GOVERNANCE RED FLAGS: HOW TO SEE THE WRITING ON THE WALL

Do your corporation's governance practices need to be tightened? It's easy to spot dishonesty after it's caused ruin or trauma within a department or a company. But it's not so easy to spot in its early stages. So how will you know if your company is beginning to get into trouble? Implementing a solid governance program is important, but you have to be on the lookout for red flags, be diligent in your review of the facts, and you have to be able to read between the lines to see the things that aren't readily apparent. Here are a few classic textbook signs that a company is in trouble:

Red Flag Number 1:
Creative, Complex, and Confusing Accounting

After the infamous Enron scandal, people said that if someone had simply looked at Enron's accounting practices (both on and off the balance sheet), it would have been obvious that the company was in trouble. But if that were true, why didn't the whistle-blowers come forward sooner, and why didn't anyone see the red flags? Enron had a code of ethics in name only, which is why no one thought to implement it at the highest levels of the company.

After Enron made headlines, executives at Adelphia were accused of similar wrongdoings. The media frenzy had started, and soon a newspaper article reported that Institutional Shareholder Services (ISS), the leading provider of proxy voting and corporate-governance services, had rated Adelphia in the lowest quartile for corporate governance. Was the financial community asleep? Were the company's directors asleep?

Here you had a respected, accessible organization that publicly rated Adelphia low on corporate governance, yet no one took this as a red flag! Adelphia was a family dictatorship that served its dictator first and foremost, and by the time an investigation was conducted, the pillaging had been done and the shareholders were left high and dry as the company filed for bankruptcy.

Complex internal accounting is just one way that companies hide problems. Sometimes a company will practice subterfuge by spinning off their least-profitable businesses to a separate corporate entity. This kind of tactic isn't illegal, and it's not necessarily a sign that the company is in trouble, but it's a red flag worth keeping an eye on.

Red Flag Number 2: Denial

The way management handles a problem can offer insight into how big the problem really is, and into management's commitment to high ethical standards. Does management deny the problems exist, ignore them, or attempt to cover them up? If the answer isn't a firm no, watch out. When I sit on a board, I always look for how management steps up to the plate on *marginal* issues. That's a telling sign of a company management's ethical posture.

When I was a member of the board at Midas, Inc. (the automotive car care shops), it seemed that management was in denial about a problem that was lurking beneath the surface. You couldn't see it unless you had a lot of experience in the automotive aftermarket, which I did, from my time at Quaker State. Midas had developed a parts warehouse business, and their strategy was to service independent dealers with parts on a speedy, as-needed basis. They opened forty or so warehouse stores around the country, and each had substantial automotive parts inventories, so its aftermarket customers didn't have to stock lots of parts. The Midas management kept saying how great everything was going to be, but I continued to question the concept because I could see issues with its financial viability. Eventually the company ran out of steam and nearly ran out of money until Midas had to pull the plug on it. All along the way the CEO wouldn't listen; he seemed to be in denial. The board voted unanimously to let him go. No fun . . . but necessary. The new Midas CEO came in and shut down the parts warehouse business, and the company is on the road to recovery.

Red Flag Number 3: Excessive Debt,
Inadequate Capital, or Overextended Credit

Any one of these has the potential to be fatal, but all of them combined adds up to disaster. There's an infamous video of Ken Lay, Enron's former CEO, reassuring employees that Enron is doing fine, and that it's a great investment—just before the company collapsed. I think if a leader has to spend an inordinate amount of time squelching rumors and downplaying a falling stock price, chances are things aren't as rosy as he's painting them and more than one red flag is flying in the courtyard.

A good leader will be able to see the red flags and face up to reality. He or she won't wait for a Wall Street analyst, the SEC, or an inquiring reporter to begin a probe into them. A strong, transparent leader will reveal the problem, openly address the issue (even if it hurts to do so), and get on with the problem-solving. It's not always easy to see the writing on the wall, but the earlier you do, the sooner you can start to fix the problems, and the more likely the company will survive. If there's a profitable business beneath the surface that can be rehabili- tated, and with a transparent leader at the helm, there's no reason a turnaround can't be achieved.

When red flags appear, the transparent leader identifies the prob- lem, explains what success will look like in definitive terms, and sets a timetable for completion. In other words: "When we're successful, you'll see a viable company that is growing sales X percent per year, and growing earnings Y percent per year." These kinds of targets show your employees what has to be done and how they can help, and its good corporate governance because it gives investors a chance to un- derstand the game plan and make intelligent decisions.

Taking on a new leadership position—especially in a faltering com- pany—is a lot like being a substitute teacher. You never know what you're going to get when you walk in the door, but you know for sure it will be unpredictable. There are bound to be business and gover- nance problems and mountains of other issues to deal with that aren't readily apparent.

When I joined Quaker State there were a lot of red flags. I did an interview with *Business Week* magazine and told them that if I had done my due diligence I never would have accepted the Quaker State job. What I meant was that there were so many problems, I didn't think the company could be fixed. But we did it, and we had a team of strong, committed, and energized people who made it happen. Today, at Dial, we use a lot of the same methods we did back then, because the strategy—to operate transparently—hasn't changed. It can be ap- plied in any organization.

CHAPTER SIX

THE COMMUNICATIVE LEADER

Communication is arguably the most important facet of being a transparent leader. A leader has to know how to communicate, when to communicate, and exactly what he or she is communicating in order to be effective. Communication is vital to build trust with shareholders, confidence with Wall Street analysts, and comfort with employees. Communication is everything, and it's an integral part of any executive's transparent leadership strategy. Good leaders work on becoming good communicators.

When I first started as CEO of Dial I pledged to understand the employees who worked there and what motivated them. I knew I had to be a good communicator. I had been on the Dial board as a director, so I had the advantage of knowing the former CEO and his management style, which was a lot different than mine, and I knew that the differences would be apparent to everyone. Some would meet new leadership with open arms . . . and some with resistance.

On my second day at the company I was asked to attend a national sales meeting, and it was a perfect opportunity to get to know everyone and to let them get to know me. As I awaited my turn to speak, I looked around the room at the faces before me and listened to what they had to say about sales projections, strategy, promotional opportunities, and goals for the coming year.

I didn't know many people in the room, but everyone went out of their way to make me feel welcome. Their presentations were polished, and there were a few nervous smiles in my direction. Yet as I sat there and listened, I found myself getting irritated and focusing on the fact that there were mostly men in the room. Very few women. And hardly any minorities. I looked around, thinking maybe there were people who hadn't yet arrived. But that wasn't it. There *were* mostly men, and a noticeable absence of minorities. I had worked at a lot of different companies in my life and I found it extremely odd, and the more I thought about it the less I heard what anyone was saying. I got angrier and angrier until it was finally my time to address the group.

"Next year . . ." I said slowly, "when we have this meeting again . . . there will be more minorities in the room. That's my initial objective for this group. A successful sales force isn't successful, to my mind, unless it's diverse."

The room was silent. Some squirmed in their chairs and stared at each other. The "men's club" was exposed. My message was clear.

INTERNAL COMMUNICATION

That moment was the first impression most of those employees got of me. I'm sure it didn't win me a lot of friends that day, but it was the whole truth, and I meant it. To be an effective leader you have to make your intentions clear, and that was an important part of inserting myself into the corporate culture at Dial. From that day forward I had set expectations for a new, different, and diverse employee population.

I tend to be outspoken at times, but communicating honestly is the only way to make an impact on people. It has benefits that far outweigh the risks, especially in today's world, where companies and their executives are highly scrutinized. Frequent and open communication can squelch rumors and help people understand what's going on internally, and that's important.

Communicating the vision for an organization based on ethics, integrity, and a diverse group of people is mandatory to leading transparently. You can't have a transparent organization if you aren't diverse, if you don't have high ethical standards, and if you don't reflect high integrity. And it's one big connected circle, because you can't be transparent if you don't *communicate* those things. True transparency can only come when the leader communicates the corporate mission, builds a values-based culture, and encourages a business linked to integrity.

How a leader communicates, and the effect that has on the organization, can't be underestimated, because the way a CEO is perceived by the investors, analysts, employees, and the media can be directly linked to a company's prosperity, a fact that's been proven in studies. But after the "CEO bubble" burst, it became popular to criticize communicators. Business-book authors, journalists, and the press churned out articles and books on high-profile executives who communicated frequently, any way they could, but then failed. The celebrity CEO that people loved to read about in earlier decades became the self-promoting CEO everyone suddenly loved to hate. The media criticized leaders who had appeared on the cover of *Fortune* magazine, CEOs like Hewlett-Packard's Carly Fiorina (who took a bad situation and turned it into a real plus for HP) and others. If a high-profile executive made the slightest mistake, the media was on it, criticizing everything from the method of transportation they used to how many times he or she had appeared on television. All of the self-promoting and communicating was tied to the negative returns at their companies, and articles in business magazines talked about the danger of charisma. Even today, you can go in the business section of any bookstore and find the books that were born of the charisma-bashing trend—books like *Search for a Corporate Savior: The Irrational Quest for Charismatic CEOs.*

The Charismatic Leader

So how dangerous is it to be charismatic? I think it's far more dangerous not to be. Non-charismatic leaders can hurt a company if they don't communicate well, if people don't relate to them, or if the company message isn't represented well. Charisma is important because it's a component of communication, and charismatic leaders who do media interviews can improve a company's reputation, and ultimately the bottom line.

A recent study showed that 48 percent of corporate reputation is linked to the reputation of the CEO. Wouldn't you feel more confident investing in a company with a communicative, approachable, and charismatic CEO than one with a shy, inhibited leader who couldn't effectively communicate the corporate message? When it comes to building credibility with shareholders, how information is communicated is just as important as the quality of the information. If you're a charismatic leader, communication will be easier.

Charisma simply means that you have that "something" that people like, and when people like you, they tend to listen. They like the things that you're doing, and they'll like the things your company is doing. Charisma can't be a substitute for performance or for doing things the right way, but it's a positive trait, not a negative one. Charisma can help a transparent CEO communicate even more effectively.

There are a lot of great leaders who pop up frequently in the media, appear on the cover of *Fortune* (in some cases several times), and grant numerous interviews. They talk about their business, their personal lives, their employees. People like Warren Buffett and Herb Kelleher. Those two are frequently in the media, and they both have charisma, but they're also both very likable personalities, and they have that down-home likability factor that you can't put your finger on. It's when a leader is proud, boastful, or appears to be too good-looking, too young, too slick, or just . . . too much of something, that people start criticizing. Personally, I wish people would have more of an open mind and understand that personality traits really aren't a deciding factor in an executive's success, even though charisma helps. You can be kind of shy or you can be incredibly outgoing and charismatic as long as you communicate transparently. The only trait that is certain to kill you is if you are unable to be transparent.

I can't stress enough the importance of becoming a good communicator, especially if you desire to rise to a leadership position in the corporate world. Being an effective communicator is important, and that's why I took a Dale Carnegie course early in my career, when I was in my twenties. I wasn't really a good communicator early on, and I needed to get better. I was scared to death to give a presentation to people! Communication can change the perception in people's minds, and often it's *perception* that defines reality, and what you communicate—or don't—will stick in their minds for a long time. The way a leader is perceived also affects how the employees think, feel, and relate to the company, and it affects the way they perform their jobs. It affects how they talk to customers. Being a communicative leader who is willing to listen will help build a strong perception of the company and its leadership, and a reputation for credibility. After being a dedicated Dale Carnegie student, I felt very comfortable speaking to people, and today I enjoy it more than ever.

Communicating the Importance of Diversity

One of the first things I look at when I take on a new assignment is diversity. I'm always up front with new employees about how important it is to me. I did the same thing when I was at Campbell Soup, where I told the head of the Campbell sales group that if he didn't have a female regional sales manager within a year, he wouldn't get a bonus. He quickly appointed the first female regional manager in Campbell sales history, and as it turned out, she performed so well that over time she became the most sought-after candidate for one of Campbell's larger sales regions.

At Dial, every person in the company was asked to attend a seminar on diversity, and we created a senior leadership team to focus on diversity. I took the seminar myself, because being a CEO doesn't give you the right to skip things you're asking others to do.

Diversity is a subject that a lot of people pay lip service to, but I take it very seriously and quite personally. A diverse organization is one that's broadly representative of the population and society; that means that a diverse company will be a cross section of the entire national population, not just its upper-middle-class white neighborhood. The diverse company is a mixture of *many* cultures and backgrounds, and it's stronger because of the different talents and strengths you can draw from. Diversity is an *asset,* and not just something you do to meet nationally representative quotas.

COMMUNICATING THE CORPORATE CULTURE

Communication is essential to building the culture of a corporation. The way a leader is perceived will show up in employee attitudes, and the way a leader communicates will establish the credibility of management. As a leader, it's important to work on any communication problems you may have and continually get better at speaking, motivating, and listening. You have to be able to communicate the corporate vision, and to be consistent about your desire to place values and integrity first. But you first have to understand the psychology of what drives your employees, and the things that can impact your culture.

The Desire for Power: How It Affects the Way People Communicate

Some of the biggest drivers of corporate greed are ego and power. That's why self-serving communication externally, in media interviews or press releases, is so important to a lot of executives. The phenomenon of power is worth talking about, because it's more alluring than even money for a lot of people. Power elevates an individual, even if it is only in his or her own mind. Power builds internal strength and confidence, especially for those with low self-esteem, who often feed their egos with the importance of their work, title, and status.

For an executive who is driven by a desire for power, an appearance in a business magazine or in the newspaper is like a narcotic. I've seen the quest for power drive people to do dumb things. Power gives some people a feeling of satisfaction and control, but it can be destructive to the corporation as a whole.

In Robert Greene's book *The 48 Laws of Power,* the advice is geared toward creating more power in your life. The author recommends diversion, deceit, and lying as means to get what you want. He offers such advice as: "Crush your enemy totally," "Do not commit to anyone," and, "Conceal your intentions"—advice that could lead a young executive trying to survive in today's business world to make dumb mistakes. It's scary to see a "business" book like that on the market and to envision the leaders of tomorrow embracing those principles and building their operating philosophies on them. The truth is that most seasoned executives today can see right through the manipulators. Tricks by slick operators are a lot more likely to get you a nice set of handcuffs than a nice bonus.

I mention this in my discussion about communicating to build the corporate culture because the biggest mistake any leader can make is to underestimate the driving force of power and the other destructive elements it breeds. Power doesn't just trip up high-level executives. They're the ones we read about and see on the news, but power can affect employees and managers at all levels and ultimately help destroy a culture.

If you break down what power really means and its importance to people, you start to see that power really isn't all about influence. People who are obsessed with power are first and foremost concerned with self-preservation. Decisions are made with a "what's in it for me?" mind-set, and what's right for everyone else is secondary. They'll lie to protect their power, and their power will create dissension.

Communicating to Protect Your Culture

Communicating the pitfalls of self-preservation and power has to be continual because those things can erode your culture. The first step is to create a vision and establish a contract (even if it's verbal) with employees—an agreement that says, "This is how we plan to work, and this is what we won't tolerate." You have to douse any suspicions among employees that you'll tolerate destructive elements like quests for power, greed, political advantage, fear, and retribution. They can't be part of your work environment, and you have to communicate against them.

One of the first messages I wanted to get across to Dial employees was that there were certain things that wouldn't fly in the new Dial culture. We told them right off that we had to be open and honest with each other as we embarked upon a turnaround of the company. And we were. We made a commitment to our people, and, frankly, we couldn't have achieved a dramatic business turnaround at Dial without the support of a terrific employee population. It took us about a year to build credibility and let employees know that we were straight talkers, because they were so disillusioned with previous management.

But understanding the psychology of our employees was an important part of achieving a turnaround, and we were able to fix most of the things that were wrong, like finger-pointing and assigning blame; and we were able to take care of many silent frustrations, like charging employees for parking. Paid parking in a company lot was just ridiculous, and easy to fix. How would you feel about going in to work every day if you had to pay the company to park in its parking lot? We did away with that, and today it's strictly first come first serve. There aren't any assigned spaces for executives. Frankly, it's usually not a problem for me, because I get into work at five A.M. most days.

Since I've been at Dial we've done a lot of soul searching and communicating to protect our culture, and we created the Dial Cultural Contract *together*—not as a top-down document.

The Road to Communication: It's a Two-Way Street

Communication with employees is just as important as it is in a marriage, and it has to be done more than a few times a year. Can you imagine how smoothly your marriage would go if you talked to your wife or husband only twice a year? Not very. Now, after every quarterly-earnings and business performance report, I share the same information with our employees, so they know how the company is doing and what we have planned for the future. I talk about the performance of each of our business units, the overall performance of the company, and about the progress as it relates to the employee incentive program for the year. I always give them a chance to ask questions, and we have a teleconference set up so that people in our sales offices and plants nationwide can listen in.

In 2002, when I was asked to attend the Dial annual sales meeting, once again I looked around the room at the faces. But this time, I'm happy to say, things were different. I saw a lot of women and minorities in the room. The sales group had become much more diverse. I had communicated, and they had listened. And our sales were growing faster.

In 2003, Dial's sales management team surprised me by calling me onstage to present me with a "Top Dog" award that included my own stainless-steel hot dog stand and a personalized apron. This wasn't just a little push cart but a real hot dog stand that you could use to heat hot dogs and buns. It was a great gift! It made me feel accepted and part of the sales team, rather than just some CEO sitting in a corner office, distant from employees. If you work hard to be known as a leader who communicates openly, you'll find that you're viewed as accessible, participating, and part of the team. And that's the way it should be.

When it became evident that we had exceeded our goals, changed the business culture, and turned the company around, I sent out the following memo to all employees.

To: All Dial Employees
From: Herb Baum
Date: January 7, 2003

Wow! That's the best way to describe the performance and results of The Dial Corporation and its employees in 2002. Thanks to your great work we have just completed another incredible year! We began the year with a sense of purpose and commitment, a high sense of urgency, and a laser-like focus, all of which contributed to extraordinary business results.

Looking back to August 2000, who could have imagined that by the end of 2002:

✓ We would have reduced our debt by over $400 million
✓ Purex liquid would be outselling Tide liquid at Wal-Mart
✓ Dial Corp. soap business would surpass Procter & Gamble's soap business

✓ We would have had two successive years of maximum VERC and SIP payouts
✓ Our stock price would have doubled
✓ Cultural Contract survey results would be up for all 55 questions
✓ Employee turnover would be less than 5%.

We've had two great years and here's how we did it:

We set realistic goals, we undid our mistakes, and we focused on our core businesses, the trade, and on the consumer. We reduced our debt, we improved our culture, we focused on accountability and sense of urgency, and we reduced our costs. And through VERC, you have reaped the benefits of your involvement and hard work. I congratulate you and thank you for your efforts. Please circle February 13, 2003, on your calendar for our 2002 VERC award celebration.

While what we have accomplished has by no means been easy, as we enter 2003 we will be faced with even more aggressive expectations and challenges and we must be prepared to do whatever is necessary to succeed. The reality is that 2003 will be our toughest year yet, and 2004 and beyond will not get any easier. This comes as a result of superior 2001 and 2002 results; so the bar is set much higher. The business environment is becoming increasingly competitive in all categories, we're experiencing a shrinking of our retail and institutional customer base, and we're facing increased costs in many areas of our operation. For example, in 2003, pension expenses will increase by 25% year-over-year, medical benefits by 22%, and insurance by 29%, just to name a few. These are costs that impact our competitiveness and we must overcome them with savings in other areas.

As we enter a new year, the question facing us is: "What must we do to continue and build upon our success?" Simply put, we must sell more, spend less, and earn more than we did in 2002. How?

First, we must remain focused and committed to our core businesses. Second, we must deliver upon the promise of innovation and improve our speed to market. Third, we must give ourselves a chance to succeed by ensuring that our cost structure is competitive. And we must do all this with a high sense of urgency.

We have made strong improvement in each of these areas over the past two years but we will have to do more in 2003. As a result, we will undertake a concerted effort to eliminate non-value-added activities within the company in an effort to optimize our cost structure.

We will examine organizational effectiveness to determine what areas require additional staffing and what areas require less . . . in an effort to rebalance and/or revise our organizational needs. It is best to explore these optimization projects while we are healthy . . . doing so from a position of strength. As we proceed, we will keep you fully informed. It is likely that we will need some outside assistance in this review. More to come on this. In the meantime, two final thoughts.

First, sincere thanks for your continued hard work and dedication. Second, it's important that we come out of the gate strong in 2003 . . . focused and committed with a high sense of urgency. I know you'll do your part.

Happy New Year!

It was a simple letter that thanked everyone for all they had done and reminded them of how far we had come. I sent that memo to everyone at the end of the year to let everyone know how much I appreciated all their hard work. Would they have rather received an envelope with a big bonus in it? Maybe. A bonus is great if your company performance can warrant it, and it did. Bonus checks came a month later; but a letter of thanks also goes a long way toward long-term satisfaction and loyalty, and chances are your employees will remember it. Most employees will be familiar with the accomplishments of their own team or workgroup, but they should also know what's happening in the company as a whole.

COMMUNICATION IN A CRISIS

Every company will face a crisis at one point or another, and it will have to be dealt with. Often a crisis will start as a small rumor that careens out of control. Rumors can be dangerous—like a virus that lingers and spreads until it's sickened the culture and caused a lot of damage.

If you read this and think, "Who cares if rumors spread? They'll pass!"—you'd better think again, because a single rumor can negatively impact employee morale and even your stock price. Rumors of a potential sale of your company, of accounting mistakes, organizational changes, management impropriety, or any kind of negative business news can undo years of positive image building in an instant.

The good news is that good communication can help keep rumors from spreading and boost the level of confidence others have in your company. It's a weapon against allegations, and you can fight a rumor in a lot of ways: by issuing a press release that tells the truth, by holding a press conference, or by any other means that helps explain or dispel the rumor. When you communicate, you provide facts to back up your position, and you have the opportunity to change people's minds.

I've found that my favorite way to communicate is in person, face-to-face with employees. But sometimes you have to respond to a situation quickly, and that's when a fast email, voicemail, or letter can do wonders to help clear the air. Communication in a crisis situation is not a day at the beach, but you must do it quickly and openly.

I've learned this lesson a lot of times, but one time in particular that I remember was when I was with Quaker State and we had to close down the headquarters in Oil City, Pennsylvania. We needed to find another city for the home office because there was no airport nearby and it was often costly to get employees in and out of the city, not to mention that it was near impossible to recruit good people to move to Oil

City to work in executive-level positions. But as we were going through the motions, word leaked out that we were moving the company. On one Friday morning the employees came to work dressed in black, and the town was covered in black balloons. We refer to that now as "Black Friday." We had wanted to tell our employees first, of course, but we couldn't tell them any sooner than we did, because it was considered a material event, and we had to get it approved by the Quaker State board, notify the market, and tell our various publics (including employees) at the same time. That was the right thing to do. So we planned the move, and thought it through very carefully. But it leaked out, and I learned that when a group learns about bad news and they feel as if they haven't had a hand in the communication, the result will never be good. The later you tell the employees about any change, good or bad, the more left out they feel. Thus the black balloons, the black outfits, and the black moods when the announcement finally came.

In a Crisis: Eliminate Doubt

As a longtime CEO I've had plenty of experience dealing with unpleasant issues. One occurred shortly after I joined Dial and learned that the company was embroiled in a sexual-harassment claim dating back to 1988—more than a decade before I arrived!

We moved quickly to have our attorneys settle the case and put it to rest. We also decided it was time to confront the issue head on with employees. I drafted the following memo to dispel any rumors that might threaten the kind of open culture we hoped to build, and to let everyone know that sexual harassment or discrimination wouldn't be tolerated.

To: All Dial Employees
FROM: Herb Baum
DATE: April 29, 2003
SUBJECT: **Dial Announces Settlement with the EEOC**

Today we announced we have reached a settlement with the EEOC regarding claims of harassment at the Aurora plant. This eliminates the need for a trial.

While we believe we had strong legal defenses to the EEOC claims against the Company, it was important to bring this matter to a close. Instead of looking back and questioning actions and decisions of others who are no longer with the Company, we have made a business decision to move forward, committed to the principles and ethics that are the cornerstones of the Dial we know. With this matter now behind us, all of us can focus our energy and resources on sustaining the momentum we have going with our customers and consumers and lifting the company to new levels of success.

It is important to repeat our continued commitment to the moral and business importance of providing equal opportunity and a positive work environment for all of our employees. We are not a Company that tolerates harassment of any kind. Not only is it unlawful, but it is directly contrary to our long-standing No Harassment policy, as well as Dial's Cultural Contract and Code of Ethics and Business Responsibilities that guide our decisions and actions everyday. This is a great Company with a great future, and I want to thank you for your continued support as we move forward together.

The settlement was ironed out pretty quietly, and it was an issue that should have been over and done with years before I came on board, but if I hadn't sent out that memo, who knows what kind of false impressions might have formed in employees' minds about why we had settled the case instead of going to trial. It was important to eliminate any doubt in employees' minds about the strength of our integrity and our intentions.

ENCOURAGING HONEST FEEDBACK

Part of the communication and governance plan at Dial included implementing a toll-free number that employees could call to communicate their feelings about any issue that might be bothering them. The idea is that an employee can call with a question, or to report a potential ethics violation, and the call will be handled by an independent party, which means there can be no fear of retribution. It's a great way to foster open and honest communication with your employees. Sounds like a good idea, right? Well, I thought so, at least until the first call came in and someone called to file a complaint—about me!

Apparently someone in our information-technology group thought I wasn't being up front about potentially outsourcing the IT function. He was ruffled by the fear that he'd lose his job. I had recently told the IT group something they didn't want to hear—that we were considering outsourcing information technology to Electronic Data Systems (EDS). Anytime you have news like that to deliver, the rumor mill tends to take over and people get fearful about what might happen to their jobs. Some of the employees were afraid they were going to lose their jobs, and one of them called to voice his concerns and to complain about me specifically!

As it turns out, we did outsource IT, but we also made sure in the contract negotiations that every Dial IT employee had a job with EDS for at least two years. We announced we were outsourcing the installation and implementation of SAP, an enterprise-wide information system, and that it would cost us $35 million over two years but ultimately was expected to save us about $7–$10 million per year in information-systems costs. It wasn't cheap, but it was an investment that was in the shareholders best interest long term.

But the hotline call about the EDS transaction was important because the issue came back to me as a source of employee concern, and it let me understand how one employee, and perhaps others, had been feeling. It let me in on job-loss fears that were spreading through the rumor mill. It was important to me to protect the jobs of all affected employees, but apparently they weren't all convinced.

A lot of leaders still believe in the "what they don't know won't hurt them" philosophy, but I've found the opposite to be true. It's important to encourage feedback to rein in the rumors and check the temperature of employees. It may seem a lot easier for some leaders to ignore difficult feedback rather than to confront it, but most of the time confronting it is the best way to eliminate misconceptions before it turns lethal. I think a hotline is a great way to do that because the feedback is confidential and anonymous.

Communicating Against the Rumor Mill

Every transparent leader knows you can't ignore the power of the rumor mill. You have to communicate against it continually. When I was the chairman of Quaker State, rumors began to spread like wildfire about an impending merger. It was beyond me how the rumor mill could have started so soon, because we had reached a preliminary agreement just twenty-four hours before. But once the rumors started spreading, several variations on the truth floated around. Because of the sensitive nature of the negotiations and regulatory requirements we couldn't divulge all the details of the merger until it was ready to be announced. But it reached a point where I knew we had to do something to correct it, and to get the information about the merger out there in a transparent manner, even if it was sooner than we had intended. We drafted the following memo after an article about the potential merger appeared in the *Wall Street Journal*.

> July 1, 1998
> FROM: Herbert M. Baum
> TO: All Employees
>
> Most of you must have heard or seen the article in today's *Wall Street Journal* concerning the pending merger of Quaker State with Pennzoil. Some of the "quotes" in the article questioning the rationale of the merger are either untrue or have been taken out of context.
>
> The merger will combine the best of both businesses, complement our mix of brands and services and generate major synergies and significant cost savings that we expect will have a positive impact on shareholder value.
>
> I have likened the pending merger with Pennzoil Company's downstream operations as creating the "Procter & Gamble of the automotive aftermarket industry"—an "industry powerhouse" addressing car-protection needs "from bumper to bumper, inside and out."

If you look at any industry—from banking to pharmaceuticals to transportation to food—you can see that size matters. A growing number of companies are turning to consolidation as a way to expand their markets, cut their costs and maintain their global competitiveness. Growth must come from lower costs in today's low-inflation economy.

You can be assured that your management fully supports this merger for the best interests of the future of Quaker State and its shareowners.

After the memo, the employees reacted in a lot of different ways. We didn't want to take anything for granted, and we knew there could be no harm in overcommunicating the truth, so we held an internal meeting to talk about any concerns they might have. We let them know that we intended to be transparent about the way we did things, and that we didn't have a hidden agenda or a plan to eliminate employees' jobs after the merger. In fact, we fought pretty hard to make sure employees' jobs were protected.

EXTERNAL COMMUNICATION

Some leaders communicate really well externally but not so great internally. External communication tends to be easier because it's more about telling the company story, whereas internal communication is about leading, and offering your employees openness and meaningful answers—two things that are critical to building a strong corporate culture. Some leaders don't do this well because they feel they don't have to tell the employees everything, and, as the boss, that's their prerogative. This type of managed communication policy is dangerous to the leader, the employees, and the corporation as a whole.

The dark period after the technology bubble exploded changed the way companies are valued and caused investors to tread more carefully in the market. The Internet affected businesses all over the world, and in a survey of European CEOs, 9 percent of British chief executives affirmed that 11 to 20 percent of their companies' revenues arose from some form of e-business. No doubt the Internet has changed distribution channels and the way companies do business. It's provided access to a whole new set of investors for some companies, and it's also created new challenges. Anytime you have an introduction of a new technology, your business has to adapt, and that usually extends to the way you communicate. Companies now routinely post their annual reports on their websites for shareholders and analysts to access via the Internet. But that's something no one could have imagined decades ago—your stakeholder in his pajamas accessing your financials from his living room! It would have been easier to convince some executives that they'd have satellite offices on Mars one day.

Communicating with Wall Street

Communicating with investors and analysts is critical to a company's success. It helps them understand how your business is doing and can clear up any misconceptions they might have. If you've got a complex business, communicating with analysts and investors can help them understand it better, but the communication has to be transparent and very easy to understand.

Investors buy future earnings streams with today's dollars. That means that if your stock is selling, say, for $20 a share and is expected to earn about $1.35 per share in a year, it is selling at 14.8 times forward earnings. Based on these numbers, analysts may say the company is a good value, provided the earnings estimate is met. But communication is the key, and a transparent leader will constantly tell the financial community how the company is doing against the objective to earn that $1.35 per share, every quarter, and will identify the risks associated with meeting the estimate. That's the kind of information the financial community wants and deserves.

When we do this at our company, I tend to be ultra-conservative. I don't promise anything that we don't have a near 100 percent chance of achieving (remember . . . no surprises). That's because no one can predict the future, even though we get daily sales reports that tell us how much we're selling, how much we make on what we're selling, and what our costs to sell it will be. We can predict how a quarter is going with this information, but there can also be unanticipated circumstances. Markets are fickle; world events can impact sales and earnings; competitors may do something unique that will affect your sales. Even trends can affect a business dramatically. Try being a pasta company in a low-carb world! That's when external communication and maybe even a new strategy is more important than ever. It's the leader's obligation to be clear, fast, and thorough about communicating the company's information.

Communicating externally, with analysts, shareholders, the press, and the general public is as important as communicating with employees.

Communicating with Shareholders

A good indicator of how well the leader of a company communicates is how well trust is established with shareholders, and how the shareholders perceive the company, in good times and in bad. One company that faced a rocky time but was able to preserve shareholder value and trust was Johnson & Johnson after the 1982 Tylenol scare. In October of 1982 the company faced a crisis when seven people in Chicago died after taking Extra-Strength Tylenol capsules, the leading painkiller in the United States. It was reported that an unknown suspect had inserted cyanide into Tylenol capsules and returned them, in original-looking packaging, to store shelves, where unsuspecting consumers found and purchased the tainted bottles. That year had been a strong one for Tylenol, which dominated 37 percent of its market. But immediately after the cyanide poisonings, Tylenol market share dropped to 7 percent.

Johnson & Johnson's reputation was temporarily tarnished, and shareholders bailed out of the stock left and right. But the company took an open stance and confronted the crisis head on with public announcements and communication that warned everyone about the consumption of Tylenol. Imagine having to warn your customers about buying your bread and butter!

J&J executives were faced with a serious dilemma: How to handle a crisis involving one of the company's most profitable products without permanently harming the reputation of the company or the product itself? Communication was the only answer, and they did it effectively. Johnson & Johnson executives made an immediate decision to recall the Tylenol product, which amounted to more than 30 million bottles and a loss of more than $100 million. They announced the recall and they ceased advertising for the product, and even though they weren't directly responsible for the tampering, they assumed responsibility publicly by assuring consumers that all bottles of Tylenol would be removed from store shelves. When that was done, Johnson & Johnson set about the task of damage control, by developing a campaign to reintroduce Tylenol and restore confidence to the consumer and shareholders.

J&J responded to the Tylenol crisis effectively and transparently, and Tylenol regained its position as the leading pain reliever. Executives at the company didn't respond with denial, and they didn't try to conceal evidence that the tampering had occurred. They responded openly, and took their lumps by recalling the product, and then they moved on. That quick action and honesty earned the company an even greater respect in the eyes of consumers, restoring confidence in their product.

When they reintroduced Tylenol they focused their communication on safety. The new packaging included a triple-seal tamper-resistant bottle, something the Food and Drug Administration now requires of all over-the-counter products. J&J offered a coupon to incentivize consumers to buy Tylenol, and developed an internal campaign to train two thousand of their salespeople to make presentations that would communicate to the medical community to help restore confidence in the product. The communication plan was extensive, and it ultimately benefited the shareholders.

Johnson & Johnson's openness in handling its Tylenol crisis and the positive result can be traced to its leadership, and also to its founder, Robert Wood Johnson. In the 1940s, Johnson created the company's mission statement, which specified that *the company's responsibilities were to the consumers and medical professionals using its products, to the employees, and the communities where its people work and live, and its stockholders.* This kind of philosophy and loyalty to the consumer was the key to Tylenol's brand survival. A different leader or a less transparent corporate philosophy could have resulted in the demise of a major product and brand—and maybe the entire corporation.

. . .

While Tylenol succeeded in managing its crisis, Exxon Corporation, after a crisis of their own, did not. On March 24, 1989, one of Exxon's tankers spilled eleven million gallons of oil into Alaska's Prince William Sound. The spill dramatically affected some species of animals, most notably the harbor seals, sea otters, and cormorants, which all suffered sharp reductions in their population. The oil spill affected Alaska's tourism, because the national parks, beaches, and forests were damaged. It was found that one of the crew members was unable to maneuver the ship because he was tired from working long hours, and that another, the ship's master, had been drinking. Allegations were made against Exxon for improper training and employee workload policies.

The Exxon executives reacted to their crisis a lot differently than J&J had. Exxon's spokesman answered the initial press inquiries with "no comment," which damaged the credibility of the company and made the public feel as if senior executives were concealing information. It was a defensive, closed stance, and the media lunged at Exxon, launching charges that would appear in newspapers all around the globe. Exxon chairman Lawrence G. Rawl didn't fly to Alaska until two weeks after the spill had occurred, thus sending a negative message to the public, and to Exxon shareholders, about the importance to him of the spill.

Exxon's initial response was the opposite of Johnson & Johnson's, and the company suffered for the lack of a comprehensive explanation. The memory of the Exxon oil spill lived on in consumers' minds long after it had been cleaned up.

You never know when you'll be faced with a crisis that causes you to mobilize to rebuild public and shareholder trust. I've had a lot of them throughout my career, and they always seem to come at the worst possible time—but that's the very nature of a crisis, and how you handle it can determine your future. If your corporate culture is transparent, shareholders and the public will be more willing to listen, understand, and forgive; but if management reacts defensively or is hesitant to respond, shareholders, consumers, and employees will, naturally, react with suspicion and fear.

PART THREE
EXECUTING TRANSPARENCY

Part Three is transparency in action. It's a tactical section that will help you develop strategy and processes for achieving success as a transparent leader. The chapters in this section are geared toward providing tools to help you execute a transparent business strategy.

Chapter 7, "Addressing the MVP: The Shareholder," focuses on why it's important to communicate effectively and continually with shareholders, and how to turn the share*holder* into a share*owner.* Chapter 8, "Corporate Citizenship and Branding Honesty," examines the link between being good corporate citizens and branding a culture and reputation of honesty. Chapter 9, "The Value of Transparency," shows why transparency is the only way to success. Chapter 10, "Potholes on the Road to Transparency," reviews the obstacles that can get in the way of an open culture based on integrity, and how to overcome them.

CHAPTER SEVEN

ADDRESSING THE MVP: THE SHAREHOLDER

F or a lot of companies, the period after the economic downturn that began in 2001 was all about survival. The technology bubble burst, overvalued companies watched their shares plummet, and whole industries collapsed. Executives were forced to rethink the way they conducted business, and in many ways, the corporate world was transformed.

The effects of the economic slump were widespread, impacting not only domestic markets, but global ones as well. Individual investors all over the world watched their portfolios deteriorate, and some lost their retirement funds forever. Businesses in Japan, Germany, Italy, and France were impacted as much as those in the United States, but through all of it some companies continued on course, and succeeded despite the battered economy. How did they do it?

BUILDING SHAREHOLDER VALUE WITH TRANSPARENCY

Many corporate executives who had a transparent business strategy watched from the sidelines as some of their competitors were investigated, indicted, or shut down completely. They had a plan for the good times, but it was the same plan they used to survive the bad times. It was transparent, and when other companies were hit by the storm, the transparent ones did what they had been doing all along. They continued on course, following their standards and operating according to an openly declared set of values. They didn't have to shuffle to come up with a different strategy, because they were already doing the right thing. Their shareholders benefited, and so did the employees of those companies, and the people in the communities surrounding them.

THE TRANSPARENT LEADER IS COMMITTED TO THE SHAREHOLDER

If you research many successful companies that have had sustained success, you'll find leaders who are committed to doing business transparently and releasing information to the shareholder honestly and ethically. Those leaders have the best interests of the shareholder in mind, and they know that *transparency benefits everyone,* investors included. They know that transparency is a choice, and it can't be legislated.

This point couldn't have been made any clearer in the years following the implementation of the Securities and Exchange Commission's Regulation FD (Fair Disclosure) in the year 2000. Regulation FD was created by the SEC for the investor, and the legislation requires all U.S. public companies to fully disclose material data and information that could influence investment decisions—to *all* investors at the same time. That means companies can't be selective about the information they release, can't selectively release data to analysts or insiders before events occur, and must be totally open and transparent, or risk being penalized. It's legislation that was long overdue, but in the years since Regulation FD took effect, there has been a surge of corporate scandals that were the most severe in history—WorldCom, Enron, Adelphia, and Tyco just to name a few.

Major corporations failed as a result of opaque leadership and flawed business cultures. Some of these corporations not only compromised Regulation FD, but went out of their way to violate it.

"Changing the culture that led to these problems is like turning the *Titanic* around," said Jeffrey Bronchick, chief investment officer at Reed Connor & Birdwell, a Los Angeles money-management firm.

"You have two things fighting against reform. First, you're talking about taking money away from people. Second, the way the system is set up makes changes occur slowly. Boards meet, set up committees, rule on the committee findings. It'd take a long time to approve a change in the caterer for the meetings!"

Corporate fraud and deceit caused thousands to lose their jobs, helped send the economy into a tailspin, and created a crisis in corporate America like we've never seen. What happened? The leaders of those companies weren't open and honest, and the shareholders suffered.

There's a lot of pressure on leaders to grow companies. Everyone knows it! But you can't let that pressure become a factor in the decisions you make, or it won't benefit shareowners at all.

You have to court shareowners with integrity by communicating frequently and clearly, and understanding the nature of how a shareholder buys shares of stock. The share*holder* buys shares with certain expectations and a relatively fluid time frame for these expectations to be realized, and if the expectations aren't fulfilled, they sell the stock. If the expectations are realized they either set new expectations and hold the stock until new goals are met or they sell it and move on. The share*holder* is the new reality, and it's important for leaders to understand them.

Shareholders vs. Shareowners

You can't set unrealistic expectations and expect shareholders with their fingers on the sell button to sit by and wait when these expectations aren't met. You have to set a transparent, realistic bar—one you know you can consistently jump over so that your shareholders stay with you. It's not just the numbers you achieve that's important to the investor. It's the quality of the numbers, how you achieve them, and how your shareholders were included in the process, regardless of how good or bad the journey is.

Shareholders really only reward future growth in sales or in earnings, because that's what they're investing in, and if you're smart, your strategy includes turning the shareholder into a shareowner. A share-

owner is an investor who buys shares of a company's stock to *own* for the long run. They're the best kind of investor to have because they're the long-term investor who buys the shares for consistent growth over time. The shareowner is concerned with transparency. The shareholder should be, too; but some aren't nearly as concerned about it because their expectation often doesn't depend on how transparent your business strategy is. But the shareowner *is* concerned about transparency, long-term growth, and enduring products, because they have a longer investment horizon. If your company isn't transparent, they may feel the future is not so bright. You have to court your shareholders with continual, transparent, communication, and maybe you'll be able to turn them into shareowners one day.

Making Changes That Benefit the Shareholder

Being transparent sometimes means big changes have to occur. When I arrived at Dial we were short on cash, so we cut the dividend in half right away. We shifted that money, which had previously been going to shareholders, toward repaying the high debt we inherited. Obviously some shareholders weren't pleased with having their dividend slashed, but we explained to them that the alternative could be much worse if we didn't repay debt as part of turning the company around. In August 2000 the company had only $9 million in cash in the bank, so there was little alternative. We were cash-strapped, and cutting the dividend was a necessary solution. We then devised a plan to stop the bleeding from the acquisitions and a joint venture that prior management got involved in. We sold the struggling acquisitions for pennies on the dollar, which although it diluted shareowners' equity in the company, was ultimately the best move, because it would make their investment in Dial more valuable in its anticipated recovery.

Communicating the Long-Term Business Strategy

In early 2002 I received a call from Klaus Morwind, the executive vice president of the Laundry Care Division for Henkel KGaA, a large German manufacturer of home-care and personal-care items, adhesives, and other things like sealants and surface treatments. Klaus mentioned that Henkel would be interested in Dial's laundry-care business to expand Henkel's presence in the United States. Henkel already owned nearly 30 percent of Clorox, and almost 30 percent of Ecolab, a manufacturer of janitorial products located in Minneapolis. Henkel also owned Duck brand tape, Loctite adhesives, and several hair-care products in the United States. Although they are a major player in the laundry-detergent business in Europe, they didn't have a foothold in the North American laundry-detergent market.

From day one, I knew that selling the Dial Corporation to the *right* company at the right price would be in the best interest of the share-owners and Dial employees, and I thought that it would be a good buy for a global company to gain a consumer-products foothold in the United States, but I didn't think it would be Henkel. After all, we had partnered with them before I arrived, and the first and last time I saw the CEO of Henkel was when I flew to Henkel headquarters in Düsseldorf to suggest terminating a joint venture Dial had with them. It was an agreement that was put together before I came to Dial, and when it was terminated, Henkel and Dial both lost millions. The Dial management team that made that deal was neither transparent nor savvy.

Needless to say, I was surprised when I received the call from the head of Henkel's Laundry Care Division, and I told him that we weren't interested in selling Dial's laundry-care business by itself. We would sell the entire company, but not pieces of it. After that conversation, Klaus Morwind continued to call me once a quarter, and it was in the summer of 2003 when he called again, this time with the news that Henkel might be interested in an acquisition of the Dial Corporation.

By November of that same year I found myself on an airplane to Düsseldorf again, but this time I stayed at a much nicer hotel, and was talking *building* rather than *tearing down.* Everyone at Henkel was upbeat and accommodating.

Since I had a German surname, they asked me where my family was from, and when I told them my grandfather had been born in Cologne, where he had been a teacher, they sent a car to drive me out there at the end of the business day to see the town. It was a forty-five-minute drive from Düsseldorf, and a gracious gesture on the part of Henkel management. During that Düsseldorf visit I met key executives in the company. I sat with Albrecht Woeste, the non-executive chairman of Henkel, in his office, and we talked for a long time. We didn't talk about money, and we didn't talk about the agreement, we talked about corporate culture, and I told him that my main interest in doing the transaction with Henkel was that the people at Dial keep their jobs. I instantly liked Mr. Woeste and his business philosophies. I felt good about Henkel.

The merger agreement was signed in Chicago on December 14. To be transparent, we felt we had to announce the transaction to Dial employees at seven-thirty the next morning, before they heard it from the media. We couldn't tell them until the agreement was actually signed, and we still had a lot of details to iron out with Henkel. But once it was inked we announced it to our employees as soon as we could. We told the employees, our shareowners, and our customers at the same time, and we held a press conference to answer any relevant questions. It didn't really come as a surprise to anyone since we had talked about the possibility of selling the company from the start of my tenure at Dial. From the beginning I thought that Dial's growth would be limited as an independent entity, and I didn't hide that belief. I announced it, and I took responsibility for setting the stage for turning the company around in a transparent way that would attract a buyer, so that Dial would be strengthened overall as a company. The Henkel transaction was a positive for Dial shareholders in a lot of ways. It breathed new life into the company and ensured its future for years to come. Later on, I was told by one of the Henkel employees that he had attended a Christmas luncheon for Henkel executives where my name was brought up. He said that they talked about me and my obsession for making sure the people of Dial were taken care of, and how they saw that as a positive. I was flattered, and happy that they took my concerns about our people to heart.

HOW TRANSPARENCY AFFECTS
THE INDIVIDUAL INVESTOR

A clear and ethical business plan will almost always survive the test of time. It can be the right strategy for all seasons, and in the best interests of investors. A poorly executed business plan that isn't rooted in core values is not only detrimental to employees and shareholders, but dangerous to the economy. It can affect every one of us.

A major company downsizing, with thousands of layoffs, can undo an entire town. A large corporation that fails due to corruption or a weak business strategy can ruin thousands of careers, gutting retirements and even destroying families in the process. Every leader and executive should feel a personal responsibility to do the right thing for the good of the team. And that team is pretty big, if you consider the people outside your corporation who could be impacted if your company fails. Your business plan and how you communicate it have to be transparent, and the way you execute it does, too.

At an independent and publicly held Dial we had a chief of investor relations who knew Regulation FD inside and out. We chose to abide by it to the letter, but we also went out of our way to be transparent in all other aspects of our company—not just reporting. Regulation FD is good because it establishes full and timely disclosure and gives public companies a set of standards to operate by. Even though I've said that you can't legislate transparency, the regulation does give companies who don't know where to start a guide, and it encourages companies in general to speak earlier, and more often, and to be more comprehensive in their reporting and disclosure. The legislation also requires companies to use plain and simple language that's understandable by the average investor, to file information according to a specific calendar, and, if required, to make interim disclosures. When a company does all of those things well, the market is able to manage its expectations, and shareholders are able to make educated, informed choices. Information isn't "timed" or withheld—it's transparent, open, and there for all to see.

.   .   .

In an earlier chapter I mentioned that when I arrived at Dial I got myself into a little hot water with employees by saying that selling the company would be in the best interest of the shareowners long term. That was true, but I also knew that it was important to let everyone know that we never strategized on a short-term plan to "fatten the turkey for Thanksgiving," so to speak, or build up the company just to sell it. Instead we developed a strategic plan that focused on growth of the core businesses, reduction of debt, and growth of operating margins. We didn't have a crystal ball, so we had no way of knowing if a sale was in our future. That meant we had to set our sights on near-term success and proceed one step at a time. We needed to reestablish our credibility with the investment community. But we didn't communicate only to large, institutional investors, we announced our intentions to everyone, so that even the small individual investor and others would know what was going on.

Transparent leaders know it's not wise to take short cuts to inflate near-term numbers to prep a company for sale—because it won't have lasting effects. It won't build value for your shareowners long term, and it won't help your employees. A lot of companies lost sight of that over the past decade as they struggled to try to stop their shares from falling as investors chased the tech stocks. When the market collapsed, shareholders went through a transformation and the metamorphosis changed the way investors bought, until companies found themselves with fewer share*owners* and more share*holders*.

Calling All Shareowners: We're a Transparent Company!

If you intend to do business transparently, it's best to shout it from the rooftops. Let everyone know that your intention is to report transparently, to offer clear and coherent information about your organization. Hide nothing, and utilize the tools available in the marketplace to maintain transparency. There are software packages that help monitor and facilitate compliance to Sarbanes-Oxley; there are companies that develop and implement shareowner reporting programs and offer best practices, and websites that serve as resources for how to communicate with investors. Learn more about your shareowners, and how to reach them, and communicate everything transparently.

Knowledge: Understanding the Business Can't Be Underestimated

A lot of executives who got themselves into trouble didn't grasp the importance of understanding their businesses. If there was something they didn't understand, they either ignored it and moved on to something else or covered it up. They underestimated the importance of knowledge.

But today knowledge is more important than ever, and you have to understand every aspect of your business if you're going to lead transparently. If you don't understand it, you have to take extraordinary measures to find the answers, and you can't stop until you do. It's *that* important.

Gaining knowledge is a crucial component of transparency, because you can't be honest about the things you can't explain. Knowledge is a big component of building value for the shareholder.

Financial Statements 101

Understanding things like the financial statement can't be left to the accountants anymore. CEOs have to step up to the plate and read, review, and analyze financial statements, and good CEOs will recognize that knowing them in depth is a great aid in communicating transparently with shareholders. Transparency builds trust and confidence with investors, so it's important to continually reinforce how clear and open you are any way you can. Easily understood financial statements are one tool for communicating that openness.

In today's corporate environment, share ownership is dominated by institutional investors that have research departments that do due diligence on companies. But even individuals tend to know a lot about a company's financial situation, and if you're the leader of a public company, or desire to be one, understanding the intricate financial details—the numbers, and how everything all adds up—is just as important as knowing your vision for the company. As the Enron debacle proved, understanding things like the intricacies of the earnings statement, balance sheet, off balance sheet transactions, and cash-flow statement is the responsibility of everyone in management.

The Earnings Statement

Transparency can be communicated in a number of ways—through words, actions, and numbers. The earnings statement is one more vehicle companies can use to communicate transparently to the share-owners.

Basic accounting tells you that one of the most important figures on the earnings statement is the total operating income (or loss) and its ratio to total revenue (net sales). This is an important statement for investors because, ideally, you want to see operating income growing, both as an absolute number and as a percentage of total revenue margin growth. That usually means that a company is growing its operating income and becoming more efficient over time by managing its costs and operating expenses. There's no ideal percentage of revenue for operating income because the target percentage varies by industry. If you're leading an organization and you don't fully understand every number on the earnings statement, balance sheet, and cash-flow statement, you can't really be transparent.

When you release financial information to the media, financial analysts, and the rest of the world, it should always be thorough and consistent. The basic message should be easy to understand and transparent to everyone. And you should explain things in detail. For instance, astute investors know how to check the notes that explain the financial statements' numbers and any significant events affecting them. They know that the financial information is useful, but they also know that not every asset and liability can be measured in accounting terms. Some companies will omit assets on their balance sheet that are hard to measure or don't result from specific past events, and those are the types of things that have to be clearly explained. For example,

Coca-Cola doesn't report the company trademark—estimated to be worth more than $50 billion—on the balance sheet. Boeing's balance sheet doesn't include the value of its vast workforce of engineers and aeronautics experts. These intangible assets can help make the market value of a successful company's stock much greater than its financial statement would indicate, which is why it's so important to communicate this information to shareholders. You're not transparent if you make them read between the lines.

REGAINING SHAREHOLDER TRUST

In 2003, when a series of scandals rocked the most trusted firms on Wall Street, the long-term investor got a serious wake-up call. Things had changed. How would an investor ever be able to trust the Street again? Investigators uncovered dubious financial activities that diluted the profits of some investors, and the reputations of some major mutual fund companies were permanently tarnished. Some mutual funds had engaged in an industry practice called market timing, in which managers used global after-hours trading opportunities to rapidly buy and sell mutual funds so they could capitalize on short-term variations between the price of a share on a foreign exchange and the value of the underlying security. Market timing was a widespread, accepted, industry practice, and in 2002 the *Wall Street Journal* reprinted a Securities and Exchange Commission report on it.

The report stated: "If an International stock fund in the United States holding Asian stocks has starting assets of $50 million and five million shares outstanding, the resulting share price, or net asset value, is $10. A hedge-fund trader sees that Asian stock prices declined 10% in the latest day's trading, meaning that the international mutual fund is likely to reduce its share price by a similar amount to $9 when it sets its next NAV (Net Asset Value) at 4pm Eastern time. But the trader also sees that since Asian markets closed hours earlier, some positive news has come out that is likely to boost Asian stocks when they reopen for trading the next day. So the trader spends $10 million to buy 1.11 million fund shares at $9 each today. If Asian shares revert to their starting level the next day, the portfolio will have assets of $60 million and the trader can sell his shares at the new NAV of $9.82. That gives the trader proceeds of $10.9 million on his $10 million investment."

I'm not a trading expert and by no means a hedge-fund trader, but a lot of people who thought they were being savvy by finding loopholes in the system (by timing the market) were operating without transparency. In their quest for more dollars, they tried to beat the system without informing investors, which is the very antithesis of transparency.

The reason investigators targeted this practice is because it hurts long-term investors. Richard Strong, the chairman of Strong Funds, a major mutual fund firm, was accused of market timing, as were several employees of Putnam Investments, one of America's largest mutual fund firms. The big lesson to be learned here is that the practice of market timing appeared to be widespread, and a lot of traders were doing it. Even the biggest, the best, and the brightest. But what they all failed to see is that even though the rest of the herd was doing it, it wasn't the right thing to do.

Bending the rules is not acceptable, and shareholders will let companies know it. In December 2000, Lucent made headlines for admitting it had overstated quarterly revenues by almost $700 million. The company had more shareholders—5.3 million—than any other public company, but its sales started to fall and it began missing earnings estimates. Lucent CEO Rich McGinn was in denial and blamed others for the company's poor performance, but it didn't save him. He was voted out and another CEO was brought in. A transparent leader courts the shareowner openly, without making overly optimistic claims or selling their soul to make the numbers. Quarterly forecasts or ambitious growth targets aren't the barometer of success; the overall prospects, health, and vitality of the company are.

At both Quaker State and Dial we inherited shareholders who had been misled and were, as a result, skeptical and angry. Prior managements had lost credibility because their predictions and promises didn't come to pass. They missed numbers quarter after quarter, and by the time I arrived I had the tough task of restoring credibility. In each case, our new management team started by painting an accurate (if ugly) picture of where the company was. We then presented a plan to correct the situation, told everyone how long it would take, and made a promise to update them regularly on our progress. We also outlined what that progress would look like, and we didn't make any promises that could not be met because of a rosy estimate. It's important to present things realistically so there's not any pressure to achieve long-term unrealistic expectations. When there's pressure to hit a number that's unrealistic, there's more of a tendency to resort to "spin" tactics or accounting trickery to make it happen. That's how a lot of people get themselves into trouble.

CHAPTER EIGHT

CORPORATE CITIZENSHIP AND BRANDING HONESTY

C orporate character is priceless. The focus on transparency has caused companies everywhere to pull back the curtain, examine what's inside, and transform from inward, guarded, self-indulgent icons of materialism to responsively open organizations built on integrity. The concept of transparency has been unveiled, and it's here to stay.

THE GOOD COMPANY

In 2003, Boston College's Center for Corporate Citizenship held a nationwide contest for MBA students, offering a $5,000 prize for the best paper on corporate citizenship. The contest, sponsored by such corporate giants as Coca-Cola, Clorox, and Prudential Financial, had the stated goal of educating the next generation about the value of corporate responsibility. The winner, Jessica Brinkman (from the University of Michigan Business School), wrote a paper titled "Does Corporate Social Responsibility Lead to Improved Financial Performance?"

Corporate social responsibility—or CSR, as it's referred to these days—is a lot more than just a concept companies implement to make themselves look good. Or at least it should be. Corporations that donate to charities are nothing new, but social *responsibility* goes beyond giving because it's about being responsible, honest, and accountable to the community you work and live in, and the people your products affect. But can corporate responsibility really make a difference?

Honesty: The Newest Corporate Asset

Before the recent period of great scandal and fraud that exposed the lack of values in corporate America, companies that used honesty and values to build brands and businesses were the exception, not the rule. They were the corporations that were founded on values and built on integrity, but they were rare, and when you read about the things they were doing it seemed a refreshing break from the typical news of deceit and greed coming from the corporate world.

But the tide has turned, and honesty is now an asset that everyone wants. Good values have become trendy, and if you don't have them, your business is doomed. Your customers want honesty, your shareholders demand it, and your analysts do, too. There's a new sense of clarity about what's right and wrong in business, and now more than ever people are exercising their rights to buy from and do business with companies that do the right thing. The new consumer is smarter than ever, and they demand accountability and truth from the companies they purchase from. There's a link between corporate responsibility and the bottom line. Corporate responsibility really does make a difference, but it has to be genuine, and it has to fit with the corporation's culture.

GIVING BACK: A CORPORATION'S RESPONSIBILITY

A strong and transparent leader understands that doing the best thing for the shareholder is much more than just reporting accurately or focusing on numbers. It involves being a responsible company with employees who understand that what you take out of the community you should put back. It means educating employees on the value of giving, and acting honestly and responsibly.

Do employees really care about all this? I think the answer is yes. I think employees do care about the kind of company they work for, and

I think they'll want to be a part of a good company that promotes good values. But being responsible and open about things doesn't mean you lose your competitive edge or ability to negotiate. People tend to get confused about the link between being nice and doing good things, on the one hand, and being competitive, on the other. But you can be both! At Dial, when we enter into negotiations with a company or step into meetings, we still have our own agenda and our own goals that need to be accomplished. We've got a strategy, and we hold it until the proper time to attain the greatest favorable impact for Dial. That's just smart business, and it doesn't mean we aren't being genuine, giving people as well. We need to be socially responsible and smart business-people at the same time. You have to have balance.

The Twenty-First-Century Leader

Fostering a culture of truth and building a reputation for honesty are weighty propositions, but the transparent leader tries to accomplish them, and he or she understands the vital role that ethics, values, and honesty can play in strengthening a company and its brand. This new leader recognizes the value of a robust economy, and how the corporation can contribute to it by doing things that transcend mere philanthropy. He or she knows how economic strength and growth in the community translates to benefits for the corporation, which in turn affects the employees, and the residents of the communities they serve. The transparent leader understands the big picture and the cycle of giving back that clearly demonstrates that corporations have a genuine obligation to the communities they work in. At Dial we have various corporate giving programs that we've put a lot of thought into, and we have a corporate culture in which employees know why that's important. We give to the community by helping nonprofit organizations and civic groups, and we do it because it makes the community a better place for everyone to live.

When I was at Campbell Soup, we worked to build a strong culture and implemented something we called the Campbell Credo—a strategy that reflected our mission for doing business with integrity. We made a commitment to be good citizens, to be honest employees, and to build brands that consumers could trust. One way we worked to achieve all of that at Campbell was through a group we dubbed internally the Dead Poets Society, an informal gathering of leaders within the largest division of Campbell Soup who met over dinner once a month to talk through issues. The name arose from a popular movie that depicted an idealistic teacher who stirred up the conformist waters of a 1950s-era prep school by inspiring his students to maintain their individual identities and follow their dreams.

At our own Dead Poets meetings, we had the Campbell North and South America CFO, our head of human resources, the head of manufacturing, and the head of sales. We met at a Hyatt Hotel in Cherry Hill, New Jersey, over dinner on a weekday night, and we started a policy of rotating the responsibility for leading the discussion, so that it wasn't dominated by any one person—especially yours truly, who at the time was the president of Campbell Soup North and South America. We wanted to distribute leadership, show no favorites, and keep it open.

The unique thing about the Dead Poets Society was that nobody there had a hidden agenda, and no one was in the running for anyone else's job. We were totally open about how we wanted to pursue our vision for a better company. It was apolitical, and it was a transparent group that shared everything. Those meetings went a long way toward building a culture of openness and honesty.

At Dial, we build those connections over coffee every morning at 6:30 A.M., when I sit with our head of investor relations, the CFO, and whoever else is in early enough to join us to openly talk about important issues. We walk down to the company cafeteria together, and we talk about things. We greet employees as they filter through the cafeteria on their way to their offices, and we get to see a lot of different people.

At Hasbro, there wasn't any Dead Poets Society to speak of, but one way I worked to create a connection with people was to maintain two offices on the Hasbro campus. Because of the way the headquarters building was set up, there were actually two physical Hasbro buildings, and the people in one were a bit disconnected from the people in the other. So I had an office in each building. I'd spend two weeks of each month in each location. Then, on some hot summer days I'd put an apron on and pull a red wagon around the hallways to serve ice cream to employees so I could get to know them better.

I believe that even the slightest things a leader can do to be visible and connect with employees will help construct a culture of people who care. You can work to build a brand that consumers trust and develop a culture of people who value integrity—but first you really have to make that individual connection. Your employees and managers have to respect you, and have to know what you envision for them. The most transparent leaders understand the importance of cultivating employees to be the leaders of tomorrow who will help distribute honesty, ethics, and transparency through the companies they work for.

Branding Honesty

After September 11, 2001, America was overtaken with a surge of patriotism. Even companies that had never been patriotic before seemed to jump on the patriotism bandwagon. Americans everywhere began buying up flags and anything red, white, and blue. Businesses posted the flag in their offices, and soon the nation experienced an American-flag shortage. Before long you couldn't find an American flag anywhere, and manufacturers had to scramble around the clock to make more!

A lot of companies were moved to do things to help the victims of September 11 because they had leaders who truly cared. At Dial we had a promotion after September 11 in which we offered our Renuzit candles with a patriotic theme and part of the proceeds from each sale went to the USO. We handed out pins to all of the employees depicting the Dial flag crossed with the American flag, in support of our country, and we followed it up a year later with a pin that said: *Dial Remembers.*

We *did* remember, and after the September 11th tragedy we collected thousands of dollars for the victims' families, even though there was already a fund-raising program in place with the United Way campaign that we were all supporting at the time. We draped our buildings with American flags, which are still there to this day. We painted the walls of our plants with flags, and we painted an American flag on the roof of one of our buildings on the flight path of the Scottsdale Airport so that people on the airplanes coming into Scottsdale would be encouraged and rejuvenated to see Dial's support. We didn't do it because we thought it would sell soap. We did it because we wanted to, and we felt it was our obligation and social responsibility to the community to show our patriotism and support.

True social responsibility transcends philanthropy, because it lies at the heart of what a company really stands for. It goes beyond just giving money.

But some companies jump on a social responsibility bandwagon because they don't want to appear as if they *don't* care. They want to be *perceived* as an honest and giving company, and they're more focused on building an image for their brand or service than they are on doing the right thing. After 9/11 it didn't take long for our nation's ad agencies to pick up on the patriotic trend, and soon it seemed that nearly every company focused its ad campaign on the sense of patriotism sweeping the country. Television commercials were filled with flags, soldiers, and an abundance of red, white, and blue. Ford ran an ad campaign that offered 0.0 percent financing on their trucks, attributing it to the tragedy in America and their desire to "keep America moving forward." It was an incentive to buy trucks, plain and simple.

Another company, Toys-'R'-Us, ran an ad campaign targeted at kids with the tag line "Make a flag, make a difference." In the ad, the company offered kids free paper and markers to draw a picture of a flag—as long as parents brought their kids into a Toys-'R'-Us store before Sunday! Is it possible any toys were sold while the children were in the stores on those visits?

Eventually, it got to the point where you couldn't turn on a television set without seeing a somber ad that capitalized on the tragedy. Some companies, like Dial, were sincere in their message because they were companies that had built their corporate cultures on values and taught employees the importance of giving back. But other companies did it without much thought at all.

The onslaught of flag-waving advertising played on people's emotions and ultimately caused some to wonder about the sincerity of some of the companies that ran those ads. Eventually the trend of patriotic ads faded away. But that's the problem with event-driven advertising. It isn't focused on who you are or what your company is all about. It's focused on how you're *reacting* in a given *situation,* and it's a knee-jerk approach.

Running campaigns to coordinate with whatever is going on in the world at the moment is fine as long as the content is true to your corporate culture. Companies that try to send messages that don't fit with what they really believe are easy to identify. Their annual reports generally read more like flowery brochures listing corporate contributions to charitable causes, and flowery accolades about awards they've received. But if you ask the management or even the CEO about the strategy behind the programs, a lot of times they won't be able to talk about the details, because they haven't led with passion.

Some company leaders truly believe in the responsible manufacturing and selling of their products, but others buy into corporate social responsibility simply because their corporate counsels have told them they have to. That may sound cynical, but it's a fact of corporate life. At Dial we try to stay current with cultural trends and we do our best to appeal to new and different markets all the time. However, we don't try to be something we're not. Our brand is secure in a values-based corporate culture, and we want the people who do business with us to know it.

The Good Company Has a Responsible Leader

There was a time when the word *responsible* evoked yawns from a lot of people, because to be responsible, in their view, was the opposite of being charismatic, visionary, or legendary. But now a lot of leaders have become "legendary" simply because of their lack of responsibility. They made headlines, but for the wrong reasons.

Being responsible, transparent, and honest is a requirement for success, and those who don't see it right away will suffer the consequences. The leader has to drive it. That can mean a lot of different things—from volunteering employees' time to serving food at homeless shelters, or donating money to underprivileged children, or even helping to fund the fight against a disease. But the desire to be socially responsible has to be genuine; otherwise it's not coming from transparent leadership but from a desire to build a brand, an image, or the *appearance* of doing good. It's calculated, not genuine.

Companies with transparent leaders feel a natural obligation to the communities they work in and to their employees. Such companies—like Timberland, which we talked about earlier—become known for doing the right thing, and it becomes a natural part of their legacy. It's not forced or contrived, and they don't have to work hard at it because it's ingrained in their culture.

If a consumer doesn't know anything about a company, there are plenty of ways to find out, whether via the Internet or traditional media, and they won't hesitate to do it. Today's consumers *expect* corporate responsibility from the companies they buy from. They follow things like human rights issues, a company's position on the environment, and the conditions products are manufactured under. In some states consumers have banned together to boycott companies or products that were made by children or manufactured in underdeveloped countries under adverse conditions.

A lot of CEOs and executives think of watchdog groups as nothing more than a thorn in their side, but most watchdog groups just want companies to be transparent in their business practices when it comes to social responsibility issues. This may mean allowing site visits, monitoring of facilities, and full disclosure of international partners and employee groups. That's what being transparent is all about. Anything that will assure the public that the company has the best intentions can ultimately have an impact on the bottom line.

Most companies will do the bare minimum and abide by regulations to keep the air and the environment clean, hire minorities and women, and adhere to basic human rights laws. But those things are *requirements under the law.* They're not the hallmarks of a socially responsible company—they're basics that should be expected of *every* company. The responsible company has a strategy built on core values. They don't violate the law, or submit to bribes. The responsible company hires locally, directing money and support back to the community; it supports diversity and is proactive about identifying any threats that their products or services may create in the environment.

When I was the new president of Hasbro, I was inquisitive about human rights issues that I had read about, because Hasbro was using factories in China. In China, it was, and still is, common for certain factories to employ minors, and I wanted to feel comfortable that Hasbro was a model for human rights. There are different categories of factories in China, so we always had to monitor the operations to make sure the people who worked there were of age and being treated fairly.

Hasbro always used the "A" factories, which are very nice and stay within the limits of the law in terms of the age of employees. The A factories are clean, and nicely maintained, and they have on-site dormitories where the employees (mostly women) live. Those factories have recreational and living facilities. The employees never leave, except during the Chinese New Year, when they go home to be with their families. When I made my first trip to China as president of Hasbro, I visited a factory called "Early Light" where I saw rows and rows of women doing very detailed work on toy action figures. I asked the person who took me on a tour of the factory why those women worked so hard for very low wages. The tour guide suggested I pick any one of the workers and ask her myself, through an interpreter. So I did. I wanted to know how the workers felt about their jobs and their lifestyle.

I chose a worker and asked her why she worked for what seemed to me to be such a small amount of money. She answered that she loved being at the factory, and she liked all of the benefits they provided her. She said she sent her wages home to her family. After four or five years, she said, she would become financially comfortable in the small village she came from, and her family would be able to open a small business there. I saw that by hiring her and using the A factory workers, Hasbro was doing a lot of good for a lot of Chinese families. It was important to Hasbro that the Chinese factories they used were A factories and that the people they had working there were treated well.

Anyone you pay to do work for you—even if it's a contracted employee five thousand miles away—is an extension of your company. You have to see that they are treated as well as an employee working in other parts of your organization would be.

The Good Company Develops Good Corporate Citizens

At Dial, we're committed to being a good corporate citizen in the communities where our employees live and work. We don't do it for show, we do it because it's our responsibility, and we've targeted specific groups that we give to in order to maximize the benefit of our efforts. Like a lot of companies, we make donations to worthy, nonprofit agencies that help children and strengthen education. We have a corporate-contributions program focused on giving to charities that help children. Personally, I am dedicated to the Juvenile Diabetes Research Foundation, which hopefully one day soon will find a cure for juvenile diabetes. Like a lot of corporations, we also work with Habitat for Humanity, helping to make home ownership possible for the working poor. Families pay for their homes through sweat-equity hours and zero-interest loans, and our employees support this program by working side by side with the new homeowners and their children to build a house. At the end of the day, it's hard to say who benefits more. This is what works for us; yet for some companies, being socially responsible may mean something entirely different.

On the international scene, the focus on corporate responsibility has grown just as much if not more than in the States. The European Union is a progressive "country" when it comes to civil rights issues, and the European Commission has joined together with the United States to create programs to improve human rights in China and other parts of the world. European and American businesses are working together on a global code of conduct that would help establish consistent ethical standards that would apply to business leaders all over the world. Some countries, like Canada, have already enacted global codes of conduct for companies headquartered in Canada, on how they must do business overseas. It's a good idea, because global codes of conduct allow for trade sanctions that could be imposed against countries with excessive human rights violations, and in that way they establish boundaries that all leaders can look to for guidance.

If there weren't any regulations at all, the bribery and fraud that's still prevalent in a lot of emerging nations would only increase, and the bad companies and unethical leaders would continue to take advantage of workers—especially those in underdeveloped countries. Companies without consciences would have no problem dumping their toxic waste into the environment untreated, and exploiting loopholes in the quest to earn higher profits. We've seen it in the past, and a lot of the corporate violators have gone unpunished because there weren't any regulations that applied to doing business in certain countries. Rules and regulations are often hard to enforce and expensive to implement; but they're valuable, and they exist to set the basic standards of behavior that will keep all of us accountable.

Despite all of this there will still be companies that do *just enough,* hiring just the right quota of females and minorities, and participating in just enough charitable activity to be considered acceptable. The only thing I can say about that is that leading transparently doesn't mean following a checklist for covering your butt. It doesn't mean contributing to a children's charity because it will score you points with shareholders, and it doesn't mean creating an advertising campaign centered around integrity just because it looks good. Being a transparent leader starts with being true to yourself. If you don't like kids or if you aren't wild about animals, don't make charitable contributions to causes that support kids or animals. If you're passionate about art, give to a museum or support an up-and-coming artists' project to help promote individual artistic careers. If you like the symphony, support the symphony. Don't support campaigns you don't believe in just because you think it looks good. That's not transparent. If your business strategy isn't sincerely centered on doing the right thing, no amount of advertising or giving will brand your company as one that is socially responsible.

If you're an open and honest person with a desire to do business the right way, you have to start by developing a solid plan that starts with your own values. If you don't have any, it's time to create them for yourself. When we sat down to create an outline for social responsibility at the Dial Corporation it looked like this:

COMMITMENT TO OUR SHAREHOLDERS

- good corporate governance
- strong corporate compliance initiative

COMMITMENT TO OUR EMPLOYEES

- strong values and cultural contract
- providing a highly ethical corporate culture
- being an equal opportunity employer
- diversity initiatives
- support of employee interest groups
- training and development/mentoring opportunities
- safety programs
- code of conduct/compliance hotline

COMMITMENT TO OUR COMMUNITIES

- monetary donations to community organizations with primary focus on children and education
- employee volunteer efforts
- matching donations to United Way
- donations of products in times of crisis and need
- protecting the environment
- support for extraordinary situations
  - September 11 victims
  - Arizona forest-fire victims
- membership in public organizations
  - Greater Phoenix Economic Council
  - Greater Phoenix Chamber of Commerce
  - Violence Prevention Institute

COMMITMENT TO OUR PARTNERS/VENDORS

- Diversity Supplier Program
- protecting privacy of data

COMMITMENT TO OUR CUSTOMERS

- providing safe, high-quality products
- exceeding, not just meeting, legal and regulatory requirements

I believe the very last line of the objectives we listed, says it all. *Exceeding,* not just meeting, legal and regulatory requirements. That's the definition of good corporate citizenship. Being a giver in the community instead of a taker and formalizing your giving process so your employees have specific guidelines for giving is important. It means doing the right thing, all of the time, and creating an action plan to be responsible to the communities and people you serve.

Where Do You Start?

If your business unit, organization, or company doesn't already have a plan for being socially responsible, start by defining what social responsibility and "doing the right thing" mean to your business, and how your particular group or company can best implement a program. This may involve setting up employee brainstorming sessions. It may involve doing an internal campaign via email to solicit ideas from employees.

When you decide whom to give to, or where employees should volunteer their time, set boundaries around it, and establish specific restrictions on funding. If, for example, you're never going to support a political group or candidate, make that clear early on by establishing a set of rules. If it's practical, create employee contribution committees to make the decisions on where giving should be directed, and recruit employees from different parts of the company. And the CEO and upper-level management shouldn't be on the committee—it has to be left up to the employees.

Dial isn't a huge corporation, but we've got committees located at our manufacturing facilities and also at corporate headquarters to guide donation decisions for their respective locales. This has allowed us to support a broad spectrum of programs—like a summer camp for underprivileged youth, the Juvenile Diabetes Research Foundation, the Boys and Girls Clubs of Arizona, children's museums, minority outreach projects in various cities, and numerous other health-awareness and education programs. Empowering your employees to make decisions about how to give back will strengthen your company's standing in the community.

BUILDING A BRAND OF INTEGRITY

The best way to build integrity is to build a good corporate culture. And that starts with people. A good leader doesn't have to be told that employees drive the enterprise. He or she already knows that it's the day-to-day decisions that count, not just the big decisions made at the higher levels of the company. When you take on the perspective that it's people, not processes, that run a company, it's easy to see the importance of developing the integrity of employees. If that happens, the employees will know when the processes are flawed, and will be willing to point it out. But if the morale of employees is low and the processes are flawed, the processes will continue to be flawed until the company fails. A good example of that was Enron, where a lot of the basic processes were flawed, and a lot of different individuals allowed it to continue, even when red flags were easily visible.

Strengthening integrity in an organization is a good objective, but it's a long-term process; it won't happen overnight. It's interesting to see corporations spend millions of dollars on sales training, computer training, and diversity training (mainly as a CYA measure) yet not give any resources to an ethical training program. Integrity training should be among the priorities at any company—public or private—and should be promoted from the first day an employee starts. It can't be a once-a-year training program. It has to be something that's distributed to everyone, either via the Web or in a classroom setting, and it has to be required. Integrity isn't optional, and training for it should be offered continually throughout an employee's career.

Corporations go to extremes to protect their brand, but sometimes they forget that creating a culture of integrity is the first step. A brand is what the public feels and thinks about a company. It's what the public *sees,* what the public perceives, and eventually what the public *buys.* This is why companies spend millions of dollars and a lot of intellectual capital building brands, trademarks, and services.

The Sabre Group, based in Solana, Texas, has a brand-management process that's very specific. The rules surrounding what an employee can or cannot do are stringent, and they're outlined in a manual on the company's intranet for employees to read. If someone in a department wants to print an external promotional piece, Sabre requires they use specific fonts, and a specific color for its logo: red. And not just any shade of red. Employees can use only red number 485 for the letters that spell out the company name. When a vendor does business with Sabre, there's a brand-management meeting in advance of any contracts being signed, and if the vendor doesn't agree to stick to the brand requirements, Sabre won't do business with them. The company knows the importance of protecting its brand.

Building Relationships

A company puts its brand of honesty and integrity on the line through its actions. The best companies have built their brands and their reputations by consistently talking and listening to their customers and consumers. That's it. They're responsive, and that's how they fulfill their customers' needs. These companies are the same ones that are good at identifying needs and wants that were not being met. They know that anytime you can give someone more convenience, better service, a better price, or something that's better for them mentally or physically, you're adding value. Success will come when you can align the organization so that the top priority is anticipating and responding to the needs of your customer and consumer faster and better than your competitors. Then the consumers will recognize you as a company that delivers, and lives up to its promises. I've learned to listen to the customers and consumers over the years, and I've seen what happens when you don't.

But managing relationships means having a relationship already in place, so that if there's a problem or a hiccup somewhere along the way (and there are bound to be) the relationship is there, and your customer knows who to call. When you manage relationships effectively your customers are less likely to panic when things go wrong, because they're confident that you'll be responsive to their needs and fix the problem. Anticipation is a big part of managing a relationship, and I've found I'd rather have someone on my team with the ability to anticipate than any other skill. When you anticipate, you hear what your customers say and you act on it before they ask, you listen to their needs and you build a plan to satisfy them, because developing a better product or service is the end result of careful observation.

Over the past twenty years I've noticed a common thread running through the success of the companies I've been involved with: namely, each organization's ability to anticipate. The successful ones recognize what the consumers want and deliver it ahead of time with outstanding service. That's a component of building your company and corporate brand honestly.

CHAPTER NINE

THE VALUE OF TRANSPARENCY

On August 25, 2000, Kirk Roller, the executive vice president of worldwide sales and marketing for the Emulex Corporation, a leading developer of storage networking host bus adapters, walked into his California office to very bad news.

"Our stock just went from a hundred and thirteen dollars to forty-three cents," said his secretary.

"Yeah, right," he replied. "That's funny."

Her expression was serious. "No, really," she said. "It's true."

NASDAQ called seconds later, and it was then that Roller realized the nightmare was a reality. Earlier that morning, a false Internet News item spread through mainstream news outlets such as Bloomberg, CNBC, Dow Jones, and CBS Market Watch, stating that the CEO of Emulex had resigned and the company was being investigated by the SEC.

Emulex was a successful company. They had carved out a solid reputation in their market, and they did business with major corporations across the globe. But the false press release sent shares of Emulex spiraling downward until the company was in a crisis, losing millions of dollars of equity by the minute.

Roller told NASDAQ officials to halt trading. Within the hour reporters from every major news network appeared on Emulex's doorstep, and Roller and the other Emulex officials responded openly and honestly. They had nothing to hide.

"We have not put out a company press release today," Roller

said in a public statement. "Someone put out a release that looks like an Emulex release, using the Emulex name and logo."

When Emulex shares plummeted, the SEC and the FBI called and questioned Emulex executives about whether they knew of any disgruntled former employees or anyone else who might want to harm the company. Roller couldn't think of any. The company had done things the right way, and the culture was strong. Emulex executives immediately issued a press release stating the full truth—that the Internet report that appeared earlier in the day was a fraud, and that the company was doing great.

"The negative statements in this fictitious press release are categorically false," stated Paul Folino, Emulex's president and CEO.

Emulex had been in business for more than twenty years at the time and was a solid and profitable company. Within hours officials were able to determine that whoever had sent the false press release had also placed a trade from a computer at El Camino College in California. The individual then placed a second trade from the business center computer at the Mandalay Bay Hotel in Las Vegas, and officials tracked him to a hotel room at the Luxor, nearby. Eventually they were able to target a twenty-three-year-old former Internet News employee and former El Camino college student, Mark Jakob, as the suspect. Jakob was caught when he collected a profit of $240,000 from the hoax. But by that time, the rumor had already damaged Emulex, which lost $2.5 billion in market value in a single day.

Looking back, Roller was glad that he handled the stress of the rumor the way he always had—transparently.

"My wife and I had planned to take a vacation that day, and had booked a trip to Lake Mead. It was a devastating event for our company, but we had things under control so I couldn't see ruining our trip. We took the vacation anyway."

Most people would have canceled their vacation in the midst of a crisis like that, especially someone in the senior executive position Roller held with Emulex. But Roller knew that it was pointless to sit around and assess the damage, because they had always communicated openly with the financial community. They weren't being investigated by the SEC, and they had done everything the right way. They had worked hard to build a solid company, and he was sure that the stock price would rebound despite the hoax. Roller was right, and when trading resumed later that same day Emulex shares bounced back, regaining almost all of its value. The benefit of transparency in this instance was quick recovery.

THE VALUE OF TRANSPARENCY

Transparency can be applied in any business situation, but it's especially important in a crisis when you, your employees, and your company are most likely to be scrutinized. There's a lot of value in knowing that you have nothing to hide!

That's the freedom of being open and honest. You never have to worry about what would happen if you ended up in the newspaper, or if your company were hit with a false rumor like the one that took Emulex by surprise. When you're transparent, you shouldn't have to worry if you're investigated—because the truth is out there for all to see.

In a crisis situation, being transparent can work for you in a lot of ways, and how open you are when you initially respond—and how quickly you respond—will make all the difference in the world. Companies who haven't been totally transparent in their day-to-day operations will have a hard time hiding that fact when a crisis hits. If you're not open and honest, everyone will eventually know.

What Is Legitimate Transparency?

Genuine transparency can be hard to recognize. Some executives understand the concept of leading transparently, and their companies benefit as a result. These are the leaders who have been able to build strong corporate cultures, where doing business honestly and ethically is at the forefront of employees' minds. They manufacture and sell products that benefit the consumer and add value to their lives, and they communicate openly with shareholders, analysts, employees, and the general public.

But some companies have jumped on the transparency bandwagon just because it's fashionable in these times of business bashing. When you get on a bandwagon, be sure you know where you're going—and make sure that it's not going downhill!

Legitimate transparency occurs when an organization's goals are truly aligned with its actions, but that's hard to define and sometimes difficult to spot. The truth usually reveals itself in how your company is perceived over time. In the interest of legitimate transparency, I'd like to point out two common transparency myths.

Transparency Myth Number 1:
Dissemination of Information Is All It Takes to Be Transparent

Some company leaders buy into the notion that transparency involves nothing more than providing a lot of *information* to the public as frequently as possible. They release large amounts of information any chance they get, even if it's complex, irrelevant, or difficult to comprehend. Sometimes the information is unusually open—surrounding controversial issues or criticisms the company has received. But dissemination of information is just a small piece of being transparent, and if that's all you do, that's not good enough.

One company that has taken this concept to the extreme is Brown & Williamson, a tobacco company. Tobacco companies in general have always had staunch critics, but now some companies in the tobacco industry have decided to disseminate information about smoking and the hazards it presents to your health. It's a stance that, on the surface, seems contrary to the companies' mission and objectives.

Brown & Williamson, for example, has responded to criticism by adopting a stance completely opposite to what consumers would expect of them. If you log onto the Brown & Williamson website you'll find a "corporate responsibility" section, and when you read through it, you think this material must have been posted for their critics, not their consumers. When you click on the corporate-responsibility area you're immediately directed to a section titled: "Why don't we just stop making cigarettes?" Beneath that question is a black and white, blatant view of the company's opinions on smoking and free choice. They don't actually *say* that, on their website, but they're completely transparent with the information about how dangerous smoking is (which everyone knows anyway), and if you keep clicking, you'll find an entire area on the website dedicated to children! When you arrive at the "youth smoking prevention center" area of the website the company states: "We don't want children to smoke because there are significant health risks involved." That's being transparent, even if it's contradictory to their business mission.

It's a risky marketing position in a skeptical society where the everyday consumer is savvy enough to understand corporate missions, but the tobacco company must feel like the approach is working. They have no choice but to be transparent with their *information,* because study after study have proven that smoking can cause life-threatening illnesses and that tobacco is addictive. But by posting information that seems obvious to all of us, the company must feel as if they are in some way shaping an image of social responsibility. What else can a company that sells a product that is accused of killing people do?

If you go further into the site there's a section called "Top Secret Information," a brief item steeped in irony. "Smoking is dangerous to your health," it says. "That's it. That's the secret."

The Brown & Williamson site is more of a sarcastic tribute to their detractors, a stance they've taken perhaps because they feel they have no choice. Just about everyone believes tobacco can kill. Consumer watchdog groups, people who suffer from lung cancer, and victims' families are speaking out. Brown & Williamson has decided to be open, but that kind of disclosure doesn't necessarily equate to the true definition of transparency.

Real transparency—the kind that goes above and beyond just the delivery of information or putting on a good corporate face to the consumer—is deep, and forces whole industries to examine their business practices. It causes the pharmaceutical industry to crack down on things like counterfeit drugs, or the production of medicines that can harm consumers. It creates legislation for child-safety products, protects consumers from things like asbestos, implements laws for financial reporting, and enacts standards to protect the consumer. Whole industries are altered when transparency is legitimate and not merely situational.

Situational transparency is when a leader or company reacts openly and provides information that isn't in accord with the company's core values. Situational transparency isn't genuine. It's a grudging response to a situation or criticism, and it can't have staying power if it isn't rooted in core values. Meaning: if the entire corporate culture isn't one in which the employees understand the consequences of things like half-truths, poor product quality, or a what's-in-it-for-me attitude, the corporate culture *isn't* transparent. The company may have transparent moments, or situations in which they respond openly and ethically, but *true transparency* is different. It has staying power, and it's woven into the way employees interact, think, and live every day. It's the only kind of transparency that can have enough sustainable impact to turn a failing company around.

Transparency Myth Number 2: There's One Set of Rules
for Business and Another for Everything Else

In his book *There's No Such Thing as Business Ethics,* author John Maxwell describes a conversation that occurred one evening over dinner with the chairman and CEO of AOL Time Warner's Book Group. As they talked, the chairman looked at him and suggested that Maxwell write a book on the subject of business ethics.

"There's no such thing," Maxwell answered, and then went on to explain what we've talked about earlier in this chapter: that ethics are ethics, and that you either have them, or you don't.

Maxwell said: "There's no such thing as business ethics—there's only ethics. People try to use one set of ethics for their professional life, another for their spiritual life, and still another at home with their family. That gets them into trouble. Ethics is ethics. If you desire to be ethical, you live it by one standard across the board."

I agree with Maxwell. I hope that everyone I work with knows by now that I do business ethically, but what people don't know are the things my wife could tell you. She'd say that it's the same when I'm at home. I don't know where the root of being an ethical person comes from. Some say it's your parents, and for everyone it may be different. But even when I was growing up I was called a "goody two-shoes" because I couldn't stand breaking the rules. I've always liked to do things the right way, openly and honestly. I don't think you can separate your business and personal life when it comes to things like ethics and transparency, because you just can't fake the qualities that are such a substantial part of who you are as a person.

DO YOU HAVE A TRANSPARENT BUSINESS STRATEGY?

If you're in a leadership position you want to be sure that your employees understand your business strategy. If it's unclear, the culture will become stagnant, or chaotic, as everyone does their own thing and goes in different directions.

When we developed a plan for Dial's turnaround, we laid it all out and then did everything we said we were going to do. We reduced our debt, met our financial goals, and built market share that ultimately exceeded analyst expectations. In 2001, we raised earnings estimates three times. We didn't have to go back and make excuses for our lack of performance. Our credibility in the financial community was on the road to recovery. Our goal was simple: early on we said that we wanted to be recognized as a high-integrity company run by high-integrity people. We kept the transparency message consistent and frequent, and kept the momentum going, and our transparency in reporting paid off. The focus on exceptional customer service paid off, too, and in 2000 and 2001, Dial was awarded Wal-Mart's Supplier of the Quarter Award for *several* quarters—no small accomplishment in an industry where Wal-Mart is king!

The Importance of Trust

The most effective organizations are based on shared ethics, and that can only be possible where there is mutual loyalty, honesty, and dependability. That's why building trust is a critical component of keeping transparency alive in any organization.

I once gave a speech to a group of business-school students titled

"Trust, Integrity, and the Importance of Doing the Right Thing." In it I spoke about how it seemed as if there were no rules when it comes to our behavior as individuals, citizens, and executives. I said that doing the *right thing* is not quite as easy as it once was—mainly because there doesn't seem to be a firm consensus on what constitutes what is right and wrong.

For some people, especially college graduates who haven't had any mentors in the business world yet, the "right thing" can be hard to define. To me, the "right thing" is any action or pattern of behavior that builds trust and adds to the sum total of honesty and ethics in our society.

Political scientist Francis Fukuyama explains the importance of social capital to human development in his book *Trust*. He writes: "Social capital has major consequences for the nature of the industrial economy that society will be able to create. If people who have to work together in an enterprise trust one another because they are all operating according to a common set of ethical norms, doing business will cost less. Such a society will be better able to innovate organizationally, since the high degree of trust will permit a wide variety of social relationships to emerge."

The absence of social capital, argues Fukuyama, can have devastating consequences for an organization. "People who do not trust one another," he says, "will end up cooperating only under a system of formal rules and regulations, which have to be negotiated, agreed to, litigated, and enforced, sometimes by coercive means."

Widespread distrust imposes a kind of tax on all forms of economic activity, a tax that high-trust organizations and societies don't have to pay. In the past forty or so years, it seems we've become a more distrustful and litigious society interested in short-term payoffs. The corporate world has rewarded short-term results over character, and we're not any better off as a society because of those results. Whatever happened to managing businesses for marketplace profitability rather than what you can get in the courtroom? Even though our ancestors were exposed to fraud and a lack of integrity, our expectations and values today have multiplied the exposure many times over.

The short-term mind-set we've seen in recent years is corrupting reputations, trust, and society as a whole. Those stock analysts who promoted gravity-defying Internet companies at the same time their firms were selling those stocks to an unknowing public had to have known that that was not in the long-term interests of their clients or their own reputations. They didn't think about the importance of trust. The great god "greed" colored their thinking and actions, and thousands lost fortunes on the technology stock debacle.

The Transparent Leader Is Genuine

This trust factor also extends to your personal life, or, as Maxwell put it: "You have to be the same across the board." Most of the transparent leaders I've been acquainted with who do business ethically and value integrity are also really genuine individuals who care about doing what's right for others. You trust them because they're not the sort of egotistical dictator who sits on the sidelines and takes pleasure in catching an employee make a mistake. They're not overly emotional leaders who send nasty emails to the people that work for them when things go wrong. They're genuine people, and if you looked into their personal lives you'd probably find that they do a lot of good things for others.

The Transparent Leader Fights Evil

This title may sound a bit melodramatic, but it really is true. To be effective as a leader—and by now we've established what that means—you have to be proactive about strengthening the corporate culture and fight to neutralize anything that can threaten it. That's something that can only come from the top, because if you don't care about the bad things that can impact your employees, your shareholders, and your company, you can bet no one else will.

There are a lot of negatives that can undo all of the work you've done to turn a corporate culture in the right direction. There are schemes and rumors, which can hurt a company and gut the price of its stock in a single day, and there are fabricated allegations, lawsuits, and other surprises that can sneak up on you and your company if you're

not careful. A corporation and its CEO are prime targets for false allegations, and nearly every company in America (and/or its executives)
has been faced with bogus lawsuits at one time or another.

In my career I've seen a lot of this. I've learned that even when
you're operating your company transparently, there are predators out
there who specialize in corporate extortion that can cost your company
a lot in money and morale.

The U.S. Chamber of Commerce funded a study for the Manhattan
Institute to examine lawsuits and their consequences for corporations;
the study found that in the year 2002 alone, trial lawyers themselves
took home $40 *billion* from lawsuits against corporations. Granted,
some of the awards may have been justified, and it's the consumers'
right to protect themselves when that happens, but there are certainly
lawyers out there with marginal ethics who spend their entire careers
looking for ways to take money from corporations (clogging the system with frivolous lawsuits) simply because corporations and their
executives are "fair game."

On average, lawyers who represent plaintiffs take home 19 percent
of the settlement, and some go after corporations and individuals with
deep pockets to reap the greatest rewards. In recent years the food industry has been caught in the crosshairs, finding itself the target of
lawyers who file class-action obesity-related lawsuits. Ten years ago it
would have been hard for anyone to believe that you could sue your
favorite restaurant because you've eaten their hamburgers every week
for the last decade and now you're fat! Fighting frivolous litigation
costs corporations millions in legal fees, increased insurance premi-
ums, and revamped marketing and administrative fees; and it costs
the taxpayers—you and me—as well. Corporate leaders have to make a
personal commitment to transparency, to fight the people who make
money on false allegations, corruption, and dishonesty. Giving in to
avoid big payoffs is tempting, but it keeps the fires burning for further
legal claims. They are the invisible villains in today's business environment, and we as consumers and taxpayers ultimately wind up carrying
the load.

CHAPTER TEN

POTHOLES ON THE ROAD
TO TRANSPARENCY

I n 2000, the Bridgestone/Firestone North America Tire Company was forced into a massive product recall that had far-reaching effects. The recall, which came after widespread reports of safety concerns involving automobile accidents connected to the defective tires, involved 14.4 million Firestone tires. The Firestone tire treads reportedly separated under certain conditions, resulting in numerous deaths and hundreds of injuries, leading to the loss of millions of dollars for Firestone and a series of class-action lawsuits against the company. The tire-safety issue prompted an investigation by the National Highway Traffic Safety Administration, and Firestone eventually agreed to a proposed settlement to avoid lengthy litigation.

Under the settlement, Firestone was ordered to pay around $70 million to replace tires that were still on vehicles and then an additional $41 million to manufacture materials to comply with new safety standards. The settlement also included $15.5 million for a consumer education and awareness campaign and $19 million in attorneys' fees. The recall ended up costing them a lot more than they bargained for. When they first made the tires they didn't anticipate the problem nor the controversy that would result from it. Up until that point, Firestone had a reputation for outstanding quality. But after that, consumers questioned the safety of Firestone tires. The question was whether or not the company made safe tires—in an industry that makes products whose main requirement is keeping people safe. But the troubling part about the Firestone story is that Firestone wasn't transparent. The Firestone people reportedly knew about the tire problem as early as 1999, when Firestone initiated a tire recall in Saudi Arabia. The company then recalled tires in Venezuela and other countries; however, they never announced a formal official recall, in order to avoid having to file action with the United States Department of Transportation. Not only were they not transparent, but they were apparently devious in trying to find a way around a recall in the United States. The result? The needless deaths of men, women, and children, and a consumer boycott that prompted the Ford Motor Company, which used Firestone as a major supplier of tires, to stop doing business with Firestone altogether.

Firestone learned that events such as product recalls can destroy a brand—if you haven't been totally transparent. Unexpected events can cause major potholes on the road to success, and the threat and effects they have on a brand can be so damaging that some companies are looking at brand insurance as a measure to overcome them.

"Brand damage is one of the major business risks of the twenty-first century," says Julian James, managing director of Lloyd's North America, the North American arm of the large London-based reinsurer. "Product incidents—recalls, boycotts, scandals—can cost companies millions, affect share prices, and even result in bankruptcies."

But if a company is healthy and transparent, an unforeseen incident such as a product recall, or a contamination, won't be the end. It may take time to recover, but it won't drain you of your finances or ruin your reputation with consumers—especially if that reputation is built on trust.

During the infamous Tylenol scare, I worked at Campbell Soup Company, where we had a similar crisis, only we were able to catch it early and manage it. (Copy-cat crimes are common in corporate America, although consumers may not know it.) We received a can of our famous soup in the mail along with a note saying that the can had been contaminated with a hypodermic needle injecting poison into the can through a seam. We sent it immediately to the lab. The can appeared completely intact, the label attached and in perfect condition. You couldn't tell that it had been touched. It looked just like a regular can of soup seen on the shelf at the grocery store. When it came back from the lab we were informed that the contents had tested positive for cyanide. We had a serious problem on our hands. Someone had taken a label off, used a syringe to somehow contaminate the soup, and relabeled it.

The threat sent us into a frenzy. We pulled together all kinds of crisis-management groups to teach us how to handle the media, and the public. We thought that maybe it was a truck driver traveling from state to state who was doing it (because his letter noted that there would be contamination of our product in several states), but we couldn't be sure. Campbell cleared the shelves in many states. They did the right thing. Later on it became a problem in Canada, too, and we had to send our people into the stores there everyday to inspect the cans of soup, because we received letters from the perpetrator that said that the contaminated soup was on Canadian shelves. We knew he was capable of doing it, so we took him very seriously. In Canada we got a letter from him asking for extortion money to stop what he was doing, it was signed "Captain Teach," a reference to Edward Teach—aka Blackbeard—the Caribbean pirate who terrorized ships by boarding them, taking them over, and plundering and pillaging them. This "Captain Teach" gave us instructions for a blackmail exchange in the Canadian wilderness. We sent Dave Clark, the then president of our Canadian company and the Royal Canadian Mounted Police up to a cabin. Dave and a Mountie remained in the cabin for several days, playing cards, and anxiously awaiting word from Captain Teach.

The exchange was to occur in a canoe, on a designated date, at a prearranged time. But the exchange date came and went and no one showed. It was baffling. There were no other instances of adulterated products. Ultimately we went back to work and never heard another thing about it. A few months later a note was received at our Canadian office from the perpetrator that said: "Edward Teach is dead." Perhaps he got cold feet, having read about how the real Captain Teach had come to his death, in a trap set on a ship where the crew hid, to lure him aboard—where he was captured and beheaded. Or maybe he just decided to rehabilitate himself. Either way, that was the last we heard from that modern-day pirate.

Here's a problem with transparency. In the consumer products industry, you have contamination issues, and sometimes you run the risk of copycats, who will read about something in the newspaper and then go and do it. So you're between a rock and a hard spot when it comes to transparency with contamination, because there is no doubt you have to get the product off the shelves and make sure consumers are safe. That's first and foremost. But you also have to rely on the advisors and psychologists and people who will tell you about the copycats out there who copy the actions of the first individual trying to taint the product and harm people. Transparency is always the best way, but you have to be careful about how and what you communicate in certain situations.

We worked hard over the years to build a reputation of trust with consumers at Campbell Soup. Campbell is still a household name, and consumers know that they're getting quality every time they purchase a can of Campbell's Soup. The loyalty to the brand is overwhelming, and some adults who were raised on a particular flavor of Campbell's Soup would never consider choosing a competitive brand. That kind of brand loyalty is built over time, and it's established because of products that have consistently met consumer's expectations. Campbell's earned the consumers trust by being open, and when we were faced with a contamination issue we weren't about to let Captain Teach be victorious. When you're in the consumer-products arena you have an obligation to the consumer, to make the best products and to constantly deliver the product quality consumers demand.

We've talked about the value of transparency, and why it's important, and how to hire employees who care about people, service, and integrity. Those are the things that will save you when your business hits a pothole. But turning negatives into positives takes hard work, and it starts with the corporate culture. But you can't build a positive, values-based culture overnight.

Creating an open culture starts with the small, day-to-day tasks and employee interactions. It is based on the mission and direction set for the company, and it involves imposing that mission on employees, and directing employees who go off course to get back on the right path. Sometimes it means making hard decisions—like firing someone who just won't change their bad behavior. But you can't fire everyone, and you have to pledge to work with your employees to help them reach their potential.

The following story isn't one that I like to tell. I had to think long and hard about whether I wanted it to end up in a book for everyone to read, but in the end I decided it wouldn't really be transparent of me to omit it. It's about an experience I once faced with a good employee, an individual who, unfortunately, had a bad problem. It's a problem that was only exacerbated by the freedom that the Internet has brought with it, and it's growing so much that it exists in almost every corporation, in every corner of America. The Internet can play havoc with your corporate culture. You have to monitor it closely.

At one company I worked for, I arrived in my office early one morning to find the director of human resources standing outside my door with a worried expression. Apparently a fairly senior-level employee had been accessing pornographic websites on the Internet from the company computer. His computer had also accessed the websites of escort-services in various cities he traveled to. It was my responsibility to confront him about it, so I called him to my office for a talk. It must have been extremely uncomfortable for him, but he admitted he had a problem. He said that there were a lot of things going on in his personal life. After thinking about the solution and reviewing it with Human Resources, we decided he could stay at the company, but with several conditions attached. First, he was a senior-level employee who was due to get a very big bonus, but I docked him more than fifty thousand dollars as punishment for his behavior. We hit him where it hurt, and where he'd remember it. Why didn't we fire him? We didn't let him go because the websites he had visited didn't involve minors or any illegal behavior—just extremely poor judgment. He looked at the websites on his own time after hours, sometimes at home. In addition, he seemed to show true remorse for his actions and a willingness to change, and at work he was a valuable contributor.

A sexual behavioral problem, a problem with alcohol, or any errant behavior is tough to reprimand. You don't want to let it continue, but you do want to try to rehabilitate it. If an employee got drunk at a company party, you wouldn't necessarily fire him for it. You'd help him seek treatment first, to reform the behavior. We suggested that to the website visitor, and I made it clear that if he ever did it again he'd have to find a new job. The negative behavior had to go. It didn't fit within our corporate culture, and I let him know it. When it came time for his performance review I told him to curb his travel, since he obviously had too much time on his hands when he was on the road. A few months later at a company event, I sat and talked with his wife, and wondered what her husband was thinking as he watched us from across the room. I didn't say anything about it to his wife, and the incident was forgotten, and the employee continued to be a valuable contributor.

That scenario could have been handled a lot of different ways. We could have ignored the problem, because the employee was an important asset to the company, or we could have simply fired him. I think we handled it the right way by addressing it head on.

It wasn't fun, but I approached the employee about his problem, talked with him, and told him he'd be reprimanded. Whether he agreed with the justness of the punishment or not, it had to be done before it turned into a major issue. That kind of behavior didn't fit within the corporate culture we had created up to that point, and it couldn't be ignored. It's the daily interactions with employees, and how they're handled, that determine how effective you can be.

That's the difference between being transparent and being selective about the way you lead. With transparency, you can't avoid the unpleasant things, because you've already made a commitment to a culture of integrity and openness, and you've taken a vow to talk about the bad things that happen in your company, as well as the good ones.

DANGER AHEAD: WATCH OUT FOR THE POTHOLES

I've always been a tell-it-like-it-is kind of person, so confronting problems has never been an issue for me, but there are some people who struggle with confrontation who would rather ignore things than face them head on. That's understandable, but it's counterproductive. Sticking your head in the sand won't get you anything but a lot of grief when you finally come up for air.

Fixing problems fast is a way to short circuit the rumor mill. But how do you slay the dragons that seem to pop up every time you get things under control? There's no easy answer, because the challenges will be constant, and they'll come when you least expect it. And sometimes the things that can eat away at your culture aren't necessarily permanent problems but employee behaviors that need to be modified.

As a leader you have to realize that not every employee does things the same way you do, and you have to respect that. Unless you're the dictator of your own country you'll have to work with all sorts of behaviors and personalities.

Pothole Number 1: Mediocrity

When I worked for Campbell Soup Company, I had an employee working for me in a general-manager position (who later in his career became CEO of a company that failed under his reign, or stewardship) and he used to call me at five A.M. and talk to me about his business issues. When he worked for me, he made it sound as if he was in his office up with the roosters. Years later he confessed that he knew I was an early-morning person, so he would call me at five A.M. and act as if he were in the office, give me a complete update, and then go back to sleep! I never asked him if he was in his office, I just assumed he was. I actually admired him for his early start on the day.

He was a good employee, but he was a guy who took shortcuts. Instead of being honest with me, he found a way to capitalize on my appreciation for people who were early starters. That was his way of getting around something he didn't want to do. Cute trick, but no cigar. Not my kind of guy, and certainly not my kind of employee. But those are the kinds of habits that can hurt you in the long run. Take a hard look at anyone who consistently fails or doesn't live up to their promises and you'll probably find they've got mediocre habits and standards.

Mediocrity can hurt a company. It means settling for less than the best. I want to throw up when I see a talented person operating at half-speed . . . going through the motions . . . and collecting a paycheck. The transparent leader will set high personal standards and expect the same of others. A lot of good companies go sour because of a proliferation of mediocrity and the absence of passion.

I'm not suggesting that you have to become the next CEO celebrated on the cover of *Fortune* or *Business Week,* but I am suggesting that you take actions and develop habits that create a foundation for always doing business with integrity in order to achieve your highest expectations. That means developing intolerance for mediocrity.

Mediocrity is potent. You recognize it when you see it, and it stays with you. Another instance of mediocrity I remember was when I worked at Needham Harper and Steers and had an employee who was frequently late. He wasn't just late once in a while—he was the King of Late. He continually made excuses and took shortcuts to get things done. But because he had potential and was a good performer, his lateness was sometimes overshadowed by his good qualities. But finally, this one mediocre quality caught up with him. The final straw came when we had an important meeting and presentation to a client—the Campbell Soup Company—in Camden, New Jersey. He was the guy making the presentation, but he called and said he'd had a flat tire (while running late) on the way to the airport. He missed his flight. And lost his job. Maybe he really did have that flat tire—but by then it was a case of the boy who cried wolf. He had been definitively mediocre in the long run, because he was always running late and had no passion for his job. He was just going through the motions, and it wasn't the first time he had made excuses about why he couldn't do something he was supposed to do. By the way, it's standard operating procedure to give yourself extra time for unexpected events when you're traveling to important meetings. I had already told him that. He was fired because he had a poor attitude about being on time. It wasn't so much about the the perpetual lateness, but it seemed to me an indication of an overall lack of dedication to his work life.

Overcoming mediocrity is as important as anything else. A cover story in *Fortune* magazine reported that over 257 public companies declared bankruptcy in 2001. These were companies that had combined assets of over $250 billion, with leaders who had achieved various levels of success in the corporate world during their careers. It was an increase of 46 percent over the previous year's bankruptcies, and nearly all of them, the article claimed, were due to errors by upper management. Mediocrity may find some success in some places, but it won't lead to sustained success. It can hurt a company.

A good executive is mindful of the warning signs that can predict the onset of failure—because failure usually doesn't show up without warning. Oftentimes the warning signs are there but people don't see them because they don't want to face the facts. On the other hand, some executives are simply indifferent, too caught up in themselves. They aren't willing to take a hands-on approach to review the facts and make the necessary changes before it's too late. That's when mediocrity sets in and you run the risk of slipping into the comfort zone.

Pothole Number 2: The Comfort Zone

Getting too comfortable is a classic business error, but most people don't just fall into complacency—they slide into it slowly, after a long period of success. A number of the companies that failed were once at the pinnacle of success, but somewhere along the way they faltered. Their leaders fell into the comfort zone, stopped thinking about the importance of communicating transparently, and started to believe instead that they were so strong and well positioned in the marketplace that they didn't have to follow the rules. The comfort zone is a pothole very similar to mediocrity, because it stems from complacency, or what some would call simple laziness. When you fall into the comfort zone, you're so comfortable with what you've achieved, and so confident with where you are, that it's easy to lose sight of the importance of transparency.

Some of those companies were led by people who let the comfort of achievement trap them into believing it would always be there. Dick Grasso, whom we talked about earlier, had worked his way up through the ranks of the New York Stock Exchange over a period of thirty years, so he must have been pretty comfortable. To him, and to a lot of his colleagues, it would have been inconceivable to imagine a day when Grasso wouldn't be there, leading the Exchange. Comfort can make you forget that you have to protect what you have by always making sure you're doing the right thing.

Pothole Number 3: The Herd Mentality

The herd mentality is another pothole that can stand in the way of a transparent work culture. Employees who lean on each other, to the point where they lose their opportunity to shine independently, carry the team concept too far and run the risk of missing out on promotion opportunities. I call this the "charm bracelet effect": where one goes, everyone else goes . . . even if it's off a cliff.

I've found leadership often emerges in times of crisis, and when something goes wrong you'll see people who surprise you by stepping up to the plate and taking charge. But the opposite is also true, and you'll find those who just won't ever step up because they can't bring themselves to stray from the herd to take the big risk. The herd mentality leads employees to stay quiet when they should speak up and offer suggestions that could benefit the entire organization. Those in the herd tend to be followers, not leaders. When they become part of the herd they become docile, shy to the point of ineffectiveness.

Teamwork is good, but a herd mentality can be detrimental. It squashes creativity and prevents transparency, and it keeps people from speaking out when they suspect something is amiss. The herd mentality is very dangerous.

Pothole Number 4: Greed

Greed can be manifested in a lot of different ways, but ultimately it can be defined as compromising your integrity, honesty, and transparency for personal gain. Greed causes people to bend the rules, cover up accounting errors, and overcharge customers. Greed has caused company leaders to fudge the numbers, inflate earnings estimates, and sign off on sales figures that weren't accurate in order to make it seem as if a sales goal has been met. It's caused executives to lie and cheat to avoid having to tell a negative story about their underperforming businesses. Greed can destroy careers—but more important, it can destroy companies, too. There's no place for greed in a transparent business culture. Personally, I find it works well to surface the unpleasant issues, communicate, and address them head on.

These are the potholes you can fall into if you take your eyes off the road—mistakes like not cultivating a transparent culture, or focusing too much on a personal agenda instead of building a strong business, and so on. When your business and the marketplace around it are forced to change, new challenges emerge, and being focused on doing business with integrity is key. If you have one set of rules to turn to, it will be easier to measure success.

Greed, the herd mentality, and mediocrity are just a few of the things that can trip people up. You have to be on the lookout for them, and work to eliminate the potholes from your business culture.

Developing People

A large part of navigating the potholes and building a strong culture will involve developing employees who can spot problems and who know how to overcome them. Great leaders aren't born that way, they develop and evolve over the years, and that's why I believe in the importance of finding great mentors, and being one yourself. You have to seek out the potential in someone and develop it.

I'll never forget a time in my career when I was young and impressionable, when, in my first job, working for the public relations firm Aaron Cushman and Associates, I was asked to lead a press conference following a client's corporate meeting. The CEO ran a company I can't remember the name of, but I do remember that I was just a young person trying to get ahead in the business world. After the CEO gave his presentation, I walked up to him at the front of the room and told him that I thought he had done a great job, that he had delivered a great motivating speech. The CEO just looked down at me and said, "What do you know about anything?" I was young and inexperienced, and he let me know it in no uncertain terms.

At that moment I felt like crawling into a hole. Yes, I was just a junior person, but now, looking back, I can imagine how badly he must have treated his own people. It was a moment I won't ever forget, and an example of what not to be. If I have a chance to mentor someone today, I take it, no matter who the person is or what their title is.

If you can learn from others, you have the advantage of sidestepping grave errors and becoming a better person and leader just by observing. But there are also times when you can learn from your own mistakes. One such moment I remember came early on in my career, when I was at Doyle Dane Bernbach, a major advertising agency, and had to give a presentation in front of a packed conference room. The audience included the president of my client (the Cracker Jack Company) and Bill Bernbach and Ned Doyle, two of the agency's founders. I remember that I stood at the front of the conference room and stumbled over my words, and I doubt that anyone in the room at the time envisioned me as the future CEO of a multibillion dollar company! I performed poorly for my bosses. But the truth is, very few of us ever start out as great speakers. We begin unpolished, and it takes a while until we get polished. But that day in the conference room taught me a lesson, because I never wanted to feel that way again. I enrolled myself in a Dale Carnegie course for public speaking and ended up getting two awards in the class! That one bad business presentation experience propelled me to get better, and in a sense I was taking a leadership role over my own life and abilities. Today I'm very comfortable in front of an audience, and I'm a CEO, but it wasn't always that way. Transparency, like learning to speak well or read financials or whatever it is you want to achieve, is the same way. It doesn't come without hard work and personal commitment.

Overcoming Obstacles: Keep It Simple

When I first arrived at Dial, I asked the head of our research and development department how many projects he was working on. I was more than surprised when he said 158. Who can work on that many things at one time? I told him to work on just three, which would give him a greater focus on the areas we had interest in and be a whole lot more manageable. It didn't seem logical, anyway, to have so many ideas going, since we would have had to have funding for all of those ideas if we introduced them. We didn't have the resources for that, and what Dial needed at that time was a lot more focus and a lot less of a shotgun strategy.

When I arrived at Quaker State as the CEO, in 1993, the company was also involved in a variety of businesses—everything from automotive lubricants to warranty insurance to petroleum exploration and production, to truck and safety lighting—you name it. Quaker State was into *everything,* but it all added up to only $600 million in sales. Nearly all of the businesses were a mess, and the complexity was overwhelming. Fortunately, we were able to fix the problem in a few years.

I've heard that Enron's off-balance-sheet deals were so complex that Ken Lay and even the board of directors alleged they couldn't understand all of them. If you can't understand something, there's no way you can explain it, ethically approve it, or comprehend the impact it will have on the company. The CEO or CFO can't be the only ones who understand the business, or what drives it. At Dial, I like to think that not only do I understand our business but that our board understands our business, and hopefully our stakeholders and employees do, too . . . because of our transparency. We've taken the company back to basics, and today we have four core businesses and some great new products ready to launch.

Are your standards high enough? Overcoming obstacles means continuously evaluating where you are in order to set loftier goals for future performance. In the meantime, keep it simple.

PART FOUR
TAKING THE TRANSPARENCY OATH

In Part One of this book we talked about the power of transparency and how to build a transparent company, become a transparent leader, and hire transparent employees. We touched on the importance of transparency in today's business world and the three cornerstones of every transparent company:

1. Tell the whole truth.
2. Build a values-based culture.
3. Hire "people people."

When these three things are at the core of a company and its leadership, that's transparency in action. But a leader has to make a vow to *continue* to live transparently for the rest of the company to buy in.

In Part Two we talked about the pillars of transparency—things like corporate governance, values, and communication—and how to build a culture of integrity. In Part Three we discussed the value transparency brings to the organization. In Part Four you'll learn how to make transparency a part of everyday life, and how to make the commitment to be a truly transparent leader who will have sustained success.

CHAPTER ELEVEN

MAKING A PERSONAL COMMITMENT TO TRANSPARENCY

T his is an exciting time to be in corporate America. There's a new focus on personal values, and leaders of organizations all over the world are recognizing the link between transparency, honesty, integrity, ethics, and success.

Programs that include integrity training and building a values-based culture have become so mainstream that it's grown into an entire industry, creating a job market for those who are qualified to teach, consult, and lecture on the important mission of doing business with integrity!

It's an invigorating era to live in, and a refreshing change from the 1990s, when everything seemed to be exclusively centered on the excesses—false positives and *la dolce vita.* The nation has turned inward, and people are looking at ways to be better individuals, not just higher producers. The bottom line is still important, but so are the methods you use to achieve it.

This is an age where the current number-one book on the New York Times Best Seller List is *The Da Vinci Code,* a book about spirituality, religion, and the quest for truth. It's fiction, but even business books have taken a more personal, introspective stance, and there are other books, like *Who Moved My Cheese?* that provide answers about life and business and use morals to make a point. One of the most controversial and talked-about films in our culture was *The Passion of the Christ,* a film that looks back at events of thousands of years ago. It makes you wonder—

is all of this introspection just a passing fad, or could we really be trying to find ourselves?

IN SEARCH OF GOODNESS

I think America is tired. Tired of seeing dishonest people run companies and be rewarded for doing it. Tired of seeing the little guy
trounced on and tired of hearing about CEOs who earn thousands and
even millions more than their average employee.

In early 2004, Martha Stewart was convicted of obstruction of
justice after a trial that resulted from accusations of insider trading.
After the trial, David Kelley, U.S. Attorney for the Southern District
of New York said: "The word is beware—and don't engage in this type
of conduct because it will not be tolerated."

It was a groundbreaking judgment, because who can remember
the last time a major business figure was convicted of lying! The words
spoken by the U.S. attorney should serve notice to all of America's
leaders. This is a new era. Transparency is here to stay, and if you don't
like it, you'd better be ready to pay the price. You have to make a personal commitment to be a better person, and to live by a higher set
of values.

At the 2002 Berkshire Hathaway annual shareholders meeting,
Charlie Munger, alongside partner Warren Buffett—one of the rich-
est men in America—fielded questions from thousands of Berkshire
shareholders. When a shareholder asked about their long-term friend-
ship, Munger replied, "We've known a lot of successful businessmen
who have not one true friend on earth, and rightly so. That's no way to
live a life."

Munger and Buffett know that success in the corporate world does
not equal goodness, and that competence and intelligence aren't sub-
stitutes for ethics. They also know that leading transparently is more
than disseminating information. It's the *act* of doing well, and doing it
while you're being honest, fair, and accountable. It includes responding to criticism honorably, and taking action to right wrongs.

Business leaders who consider transparency in terms of simply following rules to comply with government regulations are missing the

boat. Executives like Warren Buffett have built reputations based on being open and honest in the way they talk, report, and conduct business. They tend to set the pace with business integrity. The Berkshire Hathaway annual report can be downloaded from the company website by anyone, and Buffett likes to say it's written in plain English. It's well worth reading because it's a refreshing change from the flowery words and half-truths often found in public-company reports.

In Search of Chaos: Why Some Executives Will Never Be Transparent

You've read about them in the *Wall Street Journal,* and you've watched them on the nightly news. You can read their case studies on the Internet, and review their long list of accomplishments and big failures by picking up a business magazine. They're executives who have failed, and you can learn a lot from them—especially from the ones who had at one point been a success.

In his book *Why Smart Executives Fail,* Sydney Finkelstein reviews several traits of highly unsuccessful executives, including: "They think they have all the answers."

That's a common attitude among people who eventually fail. If you look, listen, and observe, you'll see other bad attitudes and habits that can only lead to a dead end. There are consistent mind-sets and negative psychological traits that drive these "bad apples." Those traits can be disastrous to a company and its employees. And the most common is the absence of a personal commitment to transparency.

How many times have we heard the familiar ring of corporate buzzwords and sayings that are touted to be the Band-Aid for one corporate ill or another? Business-book gurus know that the pressure to get results is on every executive's mind and that quick answers are seductive. But sometimes the answers can't be found on paper, and the best ideas can be gained from the people around you, and those in the past. You can learn from examples of success, but sometimes there's more to learn from those who have failed.

TAKING INTEGRITY PERSONALLY

Any leader interested in bringing true change to an organization has to be able to see the link between integrity and business processes.

You can't be a transparent leader unless you make a *personal* commitment to the core principles of doing business ethically. It's not something that can be delegated to someone else. Leaders today have to take personal responsibility for enforcing and encouraging a transparent, values-based business culture. Whether you're a CEO, a middle manager, or an executive who hopes to become the next Bill Gates, making a personal commitment to transparency means you first have to: *own up to the truth; demonstrate the truth; and surround yourself with people who believe in the truth.*

Owning Up to the Truth

You may recall that when I first joined the Dial Corporation I said Dial would be better off as part of a larger corporation that had the resources necessary to develop new products and increase market share. It was the truth, and I owned up to it. I could have not said anything at all, but I came forward with a controversial statement, and I knew it would get me in hot water with some people. But when you make a vow to be transparent, you have to own up to the truth every step of the way. You can't be selective about what information you share.

Demonstrating the Truth

The rest, as they say, is history. We set about the daunting task of turning the company around and changing its corporate culture. We encouraged change where change was needed, and in the end we were successful enough to attract a buyer like Henkel, a powerful, well-run German consumer-products company. We achieved our objective, which was stated early on.

In order to demonstrate the truth and present your business in an accurate light, you have to be able to see your business objectively and understand its strengths and weaknesses. You have to know who you are and what you're capable of in order to achieve your goals as a leader, and at the same time you have to understand the organization's strengths and weaknesses to fulfill its mission.

Our vision at Dial was established early on through our cultural contract. Our goal was to do business honestly and ethically at all times, and to reap rewards for the shareholders while doing it. But before we could turn the company around, we needed to understand the advantages we had in the marketplace. We asked ourselves: What are our core strengths? Where should we focus our efforts? What should we walk from?

These are questions that every leader should ask before establishing an action plan. You can't demonstrate the truth until you know what it is, and you have to understand where your strengths lie to be able to use them to their maximum potential. Knowing your core competencies is a critical piece of taking action toward becoming transparent.

Surround Yourself with People Who Believe in the Truth

At Dial we owned up to the truth, but it wasn't just a team of managers who did it. The turnaround was achieved by every one of Dial's dedicated, hard-working employees in various departments across the company. Once we got aligned, developed the cultural contract, and started practicing transparency, nothing could stop us. We surrounded ourselves with people that believed in success through transparency. We created an environment where employees were encouraged to believe in ethical business decisions. Even today, the cultural contract we created is printed on the back of our business cards for all to see. It's a source of pride. We also have an internal business-ethics code that's distributed to all employees. Each year every one of us has to reread it and sign it all over again to establish our commitment to it. By enforcing a recommitment to the Dial Code of Ethics, we are continually fostering a corporate culture of people who believe in the truth.

It's a very real and personal gratification to look back and say that our success at Dial was large, honest, and swift. We achieved all of our goals on or ahead of schedule, and we did it the right way. When your goal is to be open and honest, your journey starts with these three things: Own up to the truth; demonstrate the truth; and surround yourself with people who believe in the truth.

MAKING TRANSPARENT DECISIONS

Whenever I'm with employees, I am reminded of my personal commitment to transparency and how it affects them.

For example, I once asked our sales team at Dial to take me to a customer to find out why they hadn't ordered one of our major new products. My original goal for the meeting was to get them to buy Zout Stain Remover, one of our newest products at the time. When we arrived at the customer, I was fidgety because I knew the product wasn't the best it could be, and I remembered that I had used the product to get a mustard stain out of my shirt and that it didn't work as well as it should have. It worked on a lot of other stains, but it didn't get the mustard out. So I told the customer to wait. I said, "I don't want you to buy this right now. I want you to wait until we get it right."

Our salesperson glared at me, and I'm sure he wanted to kick me under the table! I'm sure he probably wondered why he brought me along in the first place. He had brought me in to help make the sale, and here I was telling the customer not to buy! But it was true, and I knew if they ordered from us and their customers weren't happy that all we'd get was one order. To the sales team, it was a classic case of the CEO coming in and screwing things up! But in my eyes, transparent communication was a lot more important than any short-term result. Being honest about our product and its shortcomings would ultimately bring in a lot more business than trying to get a quick sale. Besides, it was the right thing to do.

For me, that sales call was more than a brief sales encounter. There's a fine line between what's ethical and what's transparent, because you can justify most anything if you want to. I could have justified selling the customer the product by thinking about the fact that we were continuously working on product improvements and that eventually the product would be exactly where it needed to be. But our core strength is the quality of our product, and if we have a product that isn't exactly where we think it should be . . . shouldn't we tell the customer? And why introduce it at all?

If I had tried to convince the customer to take the product, my sales team might have considered the meeting a success, but I wouldn't have been setting a good example, because it wouldn't have been completely transparent. Although the product worked well, it needed improving, and that's what I told the customer.

Making ethical decisions is perhaps the hardest part of keeping transparency alive in any organization. That's because you have to constantly take deliberate steps forward—toward an ethical mind-set, honest decisions, open dialogue, and with nothing left hidden between the lines. If you've ever been involved in a sales presentation, that's a hard expectation to live up to. But even if you're the best salesperson in the universe and are in the running for your company's top sales award for the third year in a row, it might be time to start defining yourself by how ethical and transparent your sales discussions are, rather than by how many sales you've achieved in the last quarter.

TURNING DOWN OPPORTUNITIES

I've had to analyze a lot of decisions I've made to keep myself in check and make certain they were transparent. Some of the hardest decisions you'll make in your career will involve turning down "opportunities" that come your way, but they'll be decisions you know are best in the long run.

I was asked to be a board member for KinderCare, a child-care company, and I accepted the opportunity. But later I realized that I should have turned it down. I had been recruited for the board when I was at Campbell Soup Company, after I turned down an opportunity to interview for the CEO position at KinderCare because I knew then that it wasn't something I could be passionate about—it just didn't feel right. But ultimately I accepted the board position, in large part because there were a lot of highly respected people on it. The KinderCare board members were all sharp. One of them, Geraldine Laybourne, had been the president of Nickelodeon before she founded Oxygen Media. Another, Jack Greenberg, went on to become CEO of McDonald's. It was a good board, but ultimately I resigned. I just couldn't get interested, and I wasn't contributing, and I finally resigned from the Kinder-Care board after the company had gone through bankruptcy. The whole experience was a nightmare. The board had to hire its own outside attorney to get it resolved. It taught me to do heavy due diligence before accepting a board seat. Part of your personal commitment to transparency is making sure the organizations you're involved with are up to your standards of transparency.

MAKING TRANSPARENT STATEMENTS

Most people who really know me know that on any given Saturday morning they can find me at the nearest Wal-Mart, where I like to spend a couple of hours observing consumer buying habits. It may sound strange to you, but if you were in the consumer products industry and you wanted to see what drove the consumer to buy your competitors' product, or your own, you'd spend time at Wal-Mart, too. Wal-Mart is the undeniable giant in retail sales, and when I'm there I watch people to see how they shop, and what factors might move them to make a purchase. I visit our other customers' stores, too!

Some people might find it odd that a CEO would spend his time at Wal-Mart watching what the consumer is doing, rather than staying inside the office poring over reams of reports. I do that, too, but the Wal-Mart experience just seems to me like the right thing to do, and I don't think I'd be as effective or transparent if I didn't do it. How can I make accurate statements about our products and how the consumer feels about them if I don't understand what's happening in the marketplace? I suppose I could wait for the sales or marketing team to tell me, but then I'd be getting my information secondhand.

On my first Wal-Mart excursion after joining Dial, I drove to the Wal-Mart store near my apartment in Arizona (where I live during the work week) and strolled up and down the aisle until I found the shelf displaying our detergent. The brightly colored Purex Detergent bottle stood out with its rainbow of colors, and I felt like a proud father.

There it was on the shelf. It was our product, and it stood out among the massive display of detergents.

I moved slowly, and I watched as a woman at the end of the aisle browsed the wall of detergents. Eventually she reached for one, but put it back. She picked up another bottle, opened the plastic top, and sniffed the contents. It ended up back on the shelf. Finally, the woman moved closer, stopped in front of the Purex display, opened the cap, and sniffed. She put the cap back on and placed the bottle into her cart, then walked away. I wanted to jump up and down and cheer! She had chosen our product over all the others!

Watching a potential buyer sniff a detergent bottle was important to me. For someone in the consumer-products business it was a great learning experience, especially when the product chosen by the consumer was Purex! It was a brief moment, and I'm sure one that no one else in the store noticed, but for me it spoke volumes. For one thing, I learned that consumers might just make decisions in ways that we hadn't yet considered. We had spent a lot of time thinking about things like packaging, and what's inside the bottle, and how it works, but we hadn't thought how important the fragrance of our detergents might be in the buying decision. Fragrance is important because people want their clothes to smell good as well as clean, but we hadn't put the kind of importance on it that it deserved.

The Wal-Mart visits give me a different perspective to bring back to our team at Dial. If a consumer opens the bottle, for instance, to smell what's inside before making a purchase, it could mean that introducing new fragrances is an important brand strategy, more so than even a new cleaning agent. I'm not the head of our marketing department or the chief of research and development, but I like to know what's going on in our business, and how the people who buy products make their decisions. I also spend a lot of my Wal-Mart time looking at other companies' products. I learn a lot that way.

I suppose I could take a hands-off approach and spend my Saturdays doing something more glamorous. But I feel a personal stake in the success of our company, and I want our employees to feel the same way. It also allows me to be super-transparent as a leader, because when I get in front of the customer and they ask me questions about how and why people choose our product, I don't have to give them a standard, canned response. I can give them a firsthand answer rooted in actual experience—because I've done the work required, to understand what's going on in our business.

I'm not suggesting that every employee has to go and spend their Saturday mornings at Wal-Mart watching shoppers. But if they did, it would help them understand their business better. If you're a leader, you have to set an example for your employees to follow.

THE CORNERSTONES OF TRANSPARENCY

The transparent company doesn't get that way by accident. It takes equal doses of straight talk, accountability, and openness. As we said in Chapter 1, the three principles at work in a transparent company are:

- a leader who believes in telling the whole truth
- a values-based corporate culture
- employees who are "people people"

These three cornerstones form the ideal transparent working environment, one in which the culture is positive and values-based, and where the employees are happy but not to the point of being cultish or unrealistic. The employees aren't so oblivious that they can't spot it when they stumble, and they don't carry the company banner to the point of thinking their organization is better than anyone else's.

Some corporate giants worked hard over the years to build an unfailingly positive image and work environment, mainly because positive employees who believe in you and your business are a lot easier to lead. But there's a point where team spirit can run amok, and some of these companies found that employees had such a high degree of team spirit that reality became blurred for them. Companies like IBM, to name just one, were so high on themselves back in their heyday, that the employees who worked there regarded the employees of other companies as beneath them. The culture was "we're better than you are" and it would have been difficult to change their minds. The same could be said at one time of Microsoft, and of the major airlines that refused to reduce airfares in markets they dominated. These companies developed a team-spirit atmosphere that was so overwhelmingly positive that employees turned arrogant. They wouldn't listen to their customers (because the customers needed what they had), and they wouldn't learn from others (because they were already doing it better than anyone else). That kind of corporate culture, where there's no utopia other than "our company," cannot exist for long.

In the dot-com era there was a general disdain for any of the "old" corporate models, any companies that had physical "brick-and-mortar" buildings for twenty or thirty years. The dot-coms were doing great . . . for a while. But now many of those old, traditional companies are thriving, and the dot-coms that sneered at them are long gone. The United States Army used to promote itself with the slogan "Be all you can be." That applies to your business model as well. I'd rather be a hundred-year-old redwood than a mere sapling, because there's a lot to be said for staying power. The only thing that can keep a company alive and successful for a sustained period of time is a business strategy built on transparency, integrity, and respect.

In 2003, after Dennis Kozlowski, the chief executive of Tyco International, was charged with fraud for business-related issues, more than a hundred individual buyers of fine art who were unrelated to Kozlowski or Tyco, were subpoenaed and required to pay sales tax on fine art they had purchased. These people weren't connected with the corporation or even its chairman. But after investigators began looking into Kozlowski's Tyco dealings, they found that he had also been less than transparent in his personal life. When they started digging, they found he had avoided over $1 million in sales taxes on paintings he had purchased, including a Renoir and Monet. He did it by having the art dealers ship empty boxes to an out-of-state address while the paintings were actually delivered to his (in-state) home.

The practice of avoiding sales tax on jewelry, fine art, and other expensive items isn't uncommon. There used to be a cadre of dealers and selected retailers who routinely agreed to find a way around the tax issue for some clients. It's a practice that was considered a small thing, but after Tyco, investigators in New York State began targeting individual buyers and art dealers and collected over $16 million in unpaid sales taxes. Suddenly a small thing that was generally accepted by the majority became a large issue.

If the New York art world had trained its employees to understand that tax avoidance was wrong, employees would not have gone along with customers who suggested shipping the product out of state, or any other method to avoid taxes. But the art world was simply buying into an age-old practice that too many others followed, and ultimately it cost them. Some of them found their names plastered on the front page of the *Wall Street Journal.* An awareness of and commitment to transparent business practices would have saved them.

WHAT'S YOUR LEGACY?

If you've led your life transparently, you won't find yourself, at the end of the road, looking back with regret. You'll be assured you did things the right way, most of the time anyway, and that at least your heart was in the right place.

In the business world, selling a company or turning one around always gives you a chance to reflect on what you've done, how you did it, and what you could have done better. There are always things you might want to change, but in the long run it's more important that you did things the right way while you were in the process of achieving.

It's one thing to tell the truth and establish a culture of transparency, and it's another thing to set it in motion and perpetuate that culture so it endures even after you're gone. Openness and transparency start at the top and cascade down.

Dr. Archie Dykes, a friend and fellow board member of mine who at one time was the president of the University of Kansas, is an educator and businessman who now, at the age of seventy-three, has the difficult job of managing a failing company through bankruptcy as the chairman and CEO of the Fleming Companies in Lewisville, Texas. At one point Fleming had 34,000 employees and was a successful enterprise. Archie and I sat on the Fleming board together. But now, Fleming is mired in bankruptcy and Archie is doing his best to maintain the morale of a broken company and the few employees who are left running it.

We've talked a lot in this book about how to build a positive corporate culture, but imagine trying to do it when everyone around you is losing their jobs and the company is in survival mode! Keeping ethics, integrity, and values alive is even more challenging when everyone is wondering where their next paycheck is coming from.

Archie is working hard to make certain that people keep their dignity intact while the Fleming organization struggles to sell off the pieces and emerge from bankruptcy. "It's very difficult to maintain the morale of the corporate culture in a bankruptcy," Dr. Dykes says. "People have lost their jobs, and that makes it very hard, but all you can do is try to convey the message that you understand. At Fleming there were a large number of people who were with the company for a number of years, and many of them have stayed on . . . knowing that ultimately they were going to have to leave. They are loyal to the end. But it's hard to keep morale at any reasonable level because people are losing their jobs all over the place."

Archie Dykes is a good guy who tells it like it is. He works hard to make sure the Fleming employees know they're valued, and I'm sure Fleming employees, as they depart, will be able to do so knowing that someone cared in a very transparent way.

In the excess of the eighties there was a popular bumper sticker that read: "He Who Dies with the Most Toys, Wins." It represented an era of excessive selfishness, where some kept score by the size of their boats, bank accounts, and houses. But in 2003, a billboard on the side of a country road in Texas read: "He Who Dies with the Most Toys Still Dies." A couple of decades have passed since the original bumper sticker, and the new sign reflects the new reality. Toys don't matter, and smart people don't keep score according to how much they have. They keep score by the legacy they leave behind.

I've met a lot of executives recently who really get this. They understand the concept of being real, open, and honest, and why being anything other than that is hazardous to your health and the legacy you leave in the business world and in life. But, sadly, some people who run companies are still afraid to be transparent. And if you really looked into their businesses, that's what you'd see. You'd see that a lot of their decisions are based on fear, and a lot of their strategy is built on maintaining control—for fear of what would happen if they lost it. Some of these executives are afraid of the repercussions of shareholders, and what will happen if they're open about the things that went wrong. Some people can't be transparent, because they're so afraid of what others will think if they tell the whole truth.

The erosion of values can start small, with tiny concessions—bending the rules, and the acceptance of things that might be marginal to good ethical practices. But it always starts with the individual. That's why it's so important to make a personal commitment to transparency.

Are there aspects of your life or business that aren't completely transparent? If so, it's never too late to change.

HONESTY IS THE BEST POLICY

Honesty is something that fits right in with any executable business plan. At the end of the day, you have to be able to look at your reflection in the mirror and know that you did the right thing, and that your employees did, too. I want to be known as someone who did that, and I'd like to be known as someone who really listened enough to understand what was going on.

Jack Welch once told me that the only way he could stay close to an organization as big as General Electric was to stay close to the human resources person and attend the various leadership meetings and talk with his companies' leaders. That allowed him to understand what was going on in different parts of the business. GE is a lot bigger than any company I've ever led, but it was good advice for anyone, because you can gain truth and understanding by listening, and that may mean attending a lot of different meetings in a lot of different workgroups.

When I participated in a CFO summit with Jack Welch at the end of 2003, I asked him about retirement—a scary prospect for a lot of people, including me—and I was relieved when he told me retirement was actually much better than he thought it would be. He told me not to be afraid of it, and his advice was important to me because in some ways, I was. With each year bringing me closer to the word *retirement* I had to be honest with myself and admit that I didn't really see myself sitting down in Florida on the beach reading the newspaper everyday. I'd last one day, maybe. Or a weekend, at most. But I knew I'd need more than that to keep my mind stimulated, and Jack gave me some ideas on things I could get involved in. You need that kind of fellowship, no matter what level you're at. If you wait tables or lead a company you need someone around you who has been there before, who can see things from your perspective and share ideas. If you don't do that, you have to rely on yourself for the answers, and that can feel isolating. That's what leads a lot of people down the road of fraud, deceit, and dishonesty.

HERB'S HINTS: A ROAD TO A BETTER BUSINESS LIFE

Everyone has their own way of doing things, and I'm no different. The following seven principles are truths that have guided me through my career, and helped me achieve my goals. You may like some of them and you may not like others, but they've all worked for me.

This plan is something I refer to as my Road to a Better Business Life, and it's helped me in the process of turning around some of America's greatest companies. My plan isn't based on years of surveying business leaders about their innermost thoughts, and there aren't any charts or graphs to back it up. I'm not a business consultant, nor a management guru, and I'm not even a celebrity CEO who's likely to appear on the cover of *Fortune*. But I do have more than twenty years of leadership under my belt, and these are the seven basic principles that have worked for me.

ROAD TO A BETTER BUSINESS LIFE

1. Surround Yourself with People Who Challenge You
2. Tell It Like It Is, Even if It Hurts
3. Marketing Is the World
4. Don't Fall Victim to the Popularity Contest
5. Knowledge Is Power
6. Know When to Walk Away
7. The Early Bird Really Does Get the Worm

1: Surround Yourself with People Who Challenge You

The last thing a leader needs is someone who always says "yes" to his or her ideas. Encourage people to challenge you openly, in public, and any way they want to; but if you have to challenge one of your employees, do the opposite. Do it in private so you don't embarrass them or dissuade others from challenging you. The worst kind of a leader is one who dresses someone down in front of everyone to set an example for all to see. That's just bad form, and it's not good management style, for a CEO or any executive.

At Dial we've got a section on our employee survey titled "Fear and Retribution," where people answer questions about whether or not they feel empowered to contribute and grow in the organization without fear of being criticized. The answers are important, because it's just another way we can make sure our environment remains transparent. We want to measure how employees *feel* about how open their environment is, and we want to encourage innovation without people having to worry about criticism. But it's not as easy as it sounds. You won't see much creativity unless you search out employees who anticipate and think differently than you do. If all you hire are people who are just like you, you won't get much in the way of ideas that are different from, or better than, your own.

2: Tell It Like It Is, Even if It Hurts

Good executives tell it like it is. They know that transparency can hurt, and they're not afraid of the discomfort that sometimes comes along with it. They've got courage, and they understand that great things can only be achieved through honesty, openness, and with ethics.

This rule is simple. If you made a mistake or you think you've gone in the wrong direction, admit it—and sleep better at night. This is as easy as it sounds, though it isn't for the weak of heart. The ability to fess up is a trait that every great, transparent leader possesses. It's harder to tell it like it is than it is to avoid the truth, but even when you avoid the truth, you're not fooling as many people as you think.

Pete Rose avoided the truth for a lot of years by denying that he had ever bet on baseball. But how many people really believed that he hadn't? All signs pointed in that direction, and in the end, after many years of denial, and an undoubtedly tumultuous internal struggle, he finally admitted the truth. He had bet on baseball, and he had lied about it for years. He finally came clean, but by then it was too late. He should have fessed up sooner.

3: Marketing Is the World

This rule always helps me remember one of the most important components of success for a company. And since running a company is what I've been doing for a large part of my career, I include this rule in my list to make sure it's always at the front of my mind. Outstanding marketing is what most often brings business growth and consumer loyalty, as well as increasing a company's brand recognition, making consumers aware, interested, and excited about a product. A great brand, when marketed well, is the Holy Grail of business—a lasting source of pride and profits; it's the driving force that makes your product sing. However, ineffective marketing or poor product quality can send a brand into a death spiral, causing it to disappear into the marketing graveyard.

Marketing is important because the brand lives in the mind of the customer, creating a feeling tied to an image. The man who buys Ralph Lauren for it's stature and solid feeling, the aspiring athlete who wants Adidas on his feet when he plays soccer, the housewife and amateur chef who shops at Williams-Sonoma for elegant, high-quality products, or the family who buys Dial soap for its antibacterial protection. The brand creates an impression in the mind of the consumer, drawing them into the world that is your company. Brand marketing is essential in the world of consumer products. The brand perception, whatever it may be, reflects on the leader of the company as well, and vice versa. Marketing is everything. It rules the world.

4: Don't Fall Victim to the Popularity Contest

Popularity contests are nice, but they're no way to run a business. A lot of leaders fall prey to the desire to be popular by letting bad results slide in order to remain well liked. They think, "Don't get tough, people won't like you." That kind of thought process might win you friends, but you won't keep them for long when you're in the CEO ejection seat. There has to be substance behind your strategy, and your strategy can't only be about making people like you. This was a change I had to make halfway through my business career.

I've seen colleagues of mine make dumb decisions based on their need to be liked. Mostly it comes in the form of giving poor performance one more chance—like letting key executives consistently arrive late for meetings. It shows disrespect for others' time. Now I just lock the door! Make no mistake about it. If you let mediocrity continue and strive to be liked at the expense of being a good leader, it will disrupt the objectivity and momentum of the organization. When a CEO fails to act, and fails to show personal strength and fortitude, he or she begins to lose credibility. You have to remember that you can't please all of the people all of the time. Don't try.

I lived through this at Dial when we made a business decision to shut down one of our two employee cafeterias and turn it into a fitness center. There were a lot of employees who wanted a more balanced life, and the idea of an on-site fitness center excited them. They could have lunch in the cafeteria in one building, and then walk over to the other building to work out in the fitness center when they wanted to. In the building with the fitness center we planned to have employee refrigerators so they could bring their own lunch if they wanted to, in addition to high-quality vending machines, and even a delivery service for food. We did an employee survey and the response was overwhelmingly in support of the fitness center. Yet when we shut down the one cafeteria to make room for the fitness center, we got a lot of employee complaints! We had hit a crossroads. It seemed like no matter what decision we made, someone was going to be upset.

At that point I suppose I could have tried to make everyone happy, by deciding to have two cafeterias and a fitness center, or two fitness centers, but neither would have been practical, affordable, or realistic. In the end we made the best business decision for all employees, by having one cafeteria and one workout center. Not two workout centers and not two cafeterias. One of each, where they had a choice to eat, or workout, or both! You can't please everyone all of the time, so you just have to do the best you can and forget about the popularity contest.

5: Knowledge Is Power

This rule might seem obvious, but a lot of people think they can get by on what they already know, even as things are growing and changing right in front of them.

This rule is why I spend three hours every Saturday at a Wal-Mart. I do it because I can gain a whole lot of knowledge about consumers and what they're buying, and it's a simple way to see for myself who's buying our product, as well as who's buying our competitors'. It gives me a perspective on the marketplace at the world's largest retailer, and it shows me what's going on with our competitors' products, and what's new and exciting in the world of merchandising. When I travel, I like to visit stores as part of my normal out-of-town routine. I don't have to rely on a sales report, or a monthly update to tell me what's going on. I can see it for myself. Knowledge is power. Always try to know more than the other guy.

6: Know When to Walk Away

This rule is simple, but it helps keep you focused on transparency. Know when to walk away from a situation, and remember that life's too short. You have to know when to say no. This is a skill that a lot of younger executives have a hard time with. But if you practice saying no and turning down opportunities that don't seem like positive ones for you and your company, you'll get better and better at it. It's simple: if you're involved in something that just doesn't feel right, cut the cord and walk away. Turn around early, at the first scent of trouble. Trust yourself and your gut instincts enough to know when to draw a line in the sand.

I've applied this rule many times in my career, and I've learned that sometimes you're forced to walk away from deals or people that at one time seemed attractive. And maybe they were at one point, but then it changed. That's part of anticipating and understanding when terms aren't good for you anymore. Sometimes you may be faced with having to walk away from employees who continually let you down or threaten your business, or from partnerships or investments that might be too good to be true. We faced this here at the Dial Corporation when the bankers started calling us to invest in Playtex, a company that makes sippy cups, feminine-hygiene products, and suntan lotion, among other things. The margins in most of their businesses looked good, but the business just didn't fit with our acquisition criteria. We took a close look at the business and passed on it; but later they came back to us with a more attractive proposal, and then we found ourselves faced with a dilemma. The dilemma was that the deal was attractive to the point that we found ourselves wondering if perhaps we should stretch the criteria we had established. That's called nonstrategic compromise, and ultimately we had the sense to walk away. We decided there was no way we could set outside our defined criteria, and that the deal, as good as it might be, was probably too good to be true. As it turns out, the company wasn't sold, but more importantly, the numbers just weren't right for us because they wouldn't have come close to the criteria we set to achieve success. The moral of the story? Know when to walk away.

7: The Early Bird Really Does Get the Worm

Most of the successful people I know are already awake at six A.M. Not all, but most. Say what you will, but getting up early has been proven in studies to be a basic characteristic found in successful people. I don't want to get nasty letters from all of you who don't get up until ten and still have thriving, profitable businesses, so I'll add that there are exceptions to every rule.

My own rule, however, is to get up in the dark and go home in the dark. While everyone else is still sleeping I find I can get a lot done, because once the office and the world come alive, your time is taken up with meetings and interruptions. Before normal hours is my best work time. When regular starting hours come around, that's my people time. I want to give as much time as I can to employees and outside meetings, and to do that I need to be in as early as possible to get the other things done.

I'm in the office at five A.M., Arizona time, and I'll take that time to watch the opening of the market, organize, and catch up on emails so that I've got answers by eight in the morning. I putter around and clear my head, and as it gets later I'll walk through the building and find people to talk to. I have breakfast every morning with our chief financial officer and our special assistant to the CEO, and we talk about important issues for the day. I've got a routine, but it always starts early. I believe that the early bird gets the worm. Live your business life by the clock and you'll be far more productive.

These seven principles have never let me down. They've been a road map that I've followed consistently.

PRESENTATIONS AND COMMUNICATION

This section includes examples of internal memos, letters, and actual external presentations. Communications to the outside world about the state of your company, your business objectives, and your role in the community are important facets of how a leader is perceived. Internal communications to employees and external presentations should reflect the personality of your company, appeal clearly to the audience you're addressing, and should have a clear message and point of view. Say it, and say it well.

External presentations should generally offer information about what you, your company, and your employees are all about, and how you hope to make a difference. But perhaps how you communicate internally is even more important, because when you address employees, they will always remember what you say—and they'll watch you to see if you live up to what you said.

Herbert M. Baum
Chairman, President and
Chief Executive Officer

To: Dial Employees
FROM: Herb Baum
DATE: December 15, 2003

15501 North Dial Boulevard
Scottsdale, AZ 85260-1619

Today The Dial Corporation announced that it has entered into an agreement to be acquired by Henkel KGaA, subject to Dial shareholder approval in early April of 2004. Under the terms of this agreement, Dial will become a wholly owned subsidiary of Henkel.

This is a good thing for the Company and for employees. It is the culmination of the SFX'01 strategy we put in place when I joined the Company, which said that it was in our best long-term interests to become part of a larger enterprise where we would have the resources to grow faster and compete more effectively.

This is a win/win situation for all involved. The objectives for the sale of the Company focus on insuring the profitable growth and continuity of the business and protecting the interests of our employees and our operations to the greatest extent possible.

You will notice few changes. We will remain in Scottsdale with basically the same team. I will remain CEO, the management team will stay in place and we will continue to implement our business strategies. There are no major job reductions planned, our Sales Force will stay intact, our plants will continue operating and employees will have expanded opportunities for career development as Henkel grows its presence in North America.

Henkel is an outstanding company and will bring scale, innovation and new product technologies to Dial. Dial provides Henkel with strong, healthy and growing brands as well as outstanding management and employees and a terrific growth platform in North America.

We have an incredible story to tell about how far we have come as a Company since August 2000. Our brands have never been stronger; our workforce never more committed and engaged in moving the business forward. Everyone at Dial has done a great job and I am tremendously proud of the work that has been accomplished in the last three years.

We should be proud of how we have built the business and the work we have done to turn this Company around. In fact, it is this infrastructure that you have built that Henkel is anxious to make part of its larger organization.

Regardless of a change in ownership for Dial, we must continue to work to be the best we can be and continue to be successful and profitable. We must realize that the work is not over—we must continue to build on our success and deliver our 2004 Plan. Henkel will replace our current Board of Directors as a reporting authority, and they, as did our Board, will continue to expect that we deliver results. Performance is in our control and, as our Cultural Contract states, *"we deliver on our commitments."*

We are moving rapidly to minimize any uncertainty. As this process moves forward, we will keep you informed as we have details available to help each of you understand what this decision means to you. As you have questions, send them in to *Dial Today* and we will share information as we have it available.

I encourage you to continue building on the momentum we have gained in the past three years. Our brands and our business will remain strong and successful, and becoming part of the Henkel organization will give us the resources and scale we need to leverage our strengths in the marketplace.

We know that Henkel will be a good partner—they have an exciting global presence, and the technology and resources to take our brands to the future. And we know what a great Company Dial is . . . let's continue to get the results we know we can get and show Henkel what a great decision they have made.

Herbert M. Baum
Chairman, President and
Chief Executive Officer

15501 North Dial Boulevard
Scottsdale, AZ 85260-1619

To: All Dial Employees
From: Herb Baum
Date: August 16, 2002
Subject: **Corporate Responsibility**

Throughout the past several months, with one large business after another announcing its own financial difficulties, there is an important reason I have not found it necessary to share my thoughts on corporate responsibility: You already know how strongly I feel about corporate responsibility and you have put it into practice as we operate our business every day. But as the news continues to evolve it is important that I make it absolutely clear to anyone with even a single doubt.

At Dial, we do the Right Thing. Every day. Every time. Period.

That's not a new statement for this company. The Cultural Contract, one of the first documents created by our senior leadership team after my arrival, spells out the values and behavior we expect from each member of the Dial family, whether you are dealing with a colleague or a customer. We treat people with dignity and respect. We are open and honest with each other. We deliver on our commitments. When you signed the Cultural Contract, you pledged to live up to those standards, and I pledged to hold each of you to that.

In the next few weeks, you will be asked to sign a new copy of the Cultural Contract with a ninth statement that addresses ethics directly: "We require and demonstrate ethical behavior and integrity in all our business interactions at every level in the organization." That's not a new mandate, but it is a newly stated reminder to those inside Dial and a declaration to those outside this company of how we operate and how we expect our business partners to act with us. Ethics is good for business, and is vital to the continued success of our business. Along with this note you have received a desk-top copy of the new Cultural Contract. Please use it to replace the original copy of the Cultural Contract you received in 2001 and keep it in a visible place.

In addition, each Dial employee—from the newest employee to the senior leadership team—has signed the Code of Business Conduct. That document spells out in even greater detail the behavior we expect from each person at Dial. If you have forgotten what the Code of Business Conduct says, take the time to read it again; it is available on our Intranet site and from Human Resources in hard copy form.

Financial reporting is at the core of many of the problems that have recently come to the public's attention. On that count, our financial group is strong and has high integrity leadership that we all can be proud of. Our confidence in certifying our results is high and we have filed the necessary documents with the Securities and Exchange Commission before today's deadline.

An independent Board of Directors comprised of strong business leaders also oversees Dial's management. Our outside directors have no longstanding ties to Dial management; all nine outside directors on our Board were in place before my appointment as CEO. That independence adds credibility to their oversight of the company and confidence for investors that we are performing as well as we report that we are.

When I came to Dial, I told employees that Dial's integrity as a company depends on how each one of us acts individually. I said that all of us must live up to the statements in the Cultural Contract and the Code of Business Conduct, and treat others inside and outside the company with honesty and respect.

Integrity isn't something individuals and companies can develop overnight. Individuals who demonstrate integrity will be leaders in a future that demands quality of character every bit as much as quantity of numbers. Companies that have a culture of ethics will survive today's challenges and be stronger tomorrow because of it.

THE **DIAL** CORPORATION

Herbert M. Baum
Chairman, President and
Chief Executive Officer

15501 North Dial Boulevard
Scottsdale, AZ 85260-1619

DATE: August 3, 2001
To: All Dial Employees
FROM: Herb Baum

The Board of Directors met this week to review our progress on our SFX'01 strategy and to evaluate strategic options for the Company. I promised I would update you on any news.

Today we issued a press release indicating that our strategy has been right on track. The Board realizes that we are and have been doing the right things—we've been working on fixing and stabilizing our businesses and on maximizing shareowner value.

This has been quite a year! We can count sales growth, improved gross and operating margins and an improved balance sheet among the many things on our list of accomplishments. I am so proud of all Dial employees and of all of your work and effort. Our outstanding results would not have been possible without your commitment and innovative thinking.

We continue to look ahead at what's best for the Company in the future, which may be our becoming part of a larger organization. No serious discussions for the sale of the Company as a whole have taken place, however the Board will review potential opportunities if they present themselves. We're not in any discussions with and we don't have a formal process in place to talk to potential buyers.

As I told you when we released second-quarter earnings, I will talk to you in more detail when I review the Strategic Plan with you in early September. The best thing for us to do now is to keep on doing what we have been doing: Focusing on building our core brands and businesses and continuing to improve our performance.

Good morning. I'm pleased to have the opportunity to speak to you this morning. I hope you're familiar with Dial soap—it's a brand that's been around a long time!

To make you familiar with the Company behind the soap, here's a bit of background:

- ☐ headquartered in Scottsdale, Arizona
- ☐ 2001 sales were $1.3 billion
- ☐ 2,800 employees (about 700 here in Arizona)
- ☐ manufacturing locations in the U.S., Guatemala and Argentina.

Dial has a long history of meeting customer needs and a legacy of strong brands including:

- ☐ our flagship brand, Dial soap
- ☐ Purex laundry detergent
- ☐ Renuzit brand air fresheners, and
- ☐ Armour brand food products.

I assumed the role of CEO at Dial in August 2000. My team and I found a once proud Company in steep decline. The Company had lost its way. Its strong consumer brands were in trouble. The day of reckoning was at hand and the livelihoods of scores of loyal Dial employees were on the line. What the Company needed was a fundamental cultural change that would turn this proud firm around and position it, and everyone who worked there, for a brighter future. We needed our own *"Whole New Beginning."*

In order to drive change and create the environment to support it, we had to do a lot of work to make the change take root. We got back to basics and focused on a business strategy I called "SFX'01."

- stabilizing our existing businesses
- fixing or jettisoning troubled businesses
- exploring our options as a Company

In addition, we needed to focus on the support systems and the working environment throughout the organization. Everyone was involved and an important part was a focus on Diversity because it lacked priority within the organization . . . and was a stepchild at Dial.

Diversity is not a new topic. But it's one that I'm passionate about. I believe strongly that a diverse organization—one that values and respects the uniqueness of every individual—is a stronger, more competitive organization. By fully utilizing diversity we enrich our products, our performance and our lives. The more diverse our workforce, the higher the quality of that workforce and the better able we are to:

- capitalize on new markets
- attract and retain the best employees
- increase our creativity and productivity

In other words, we're stronger, more competitive and more likely to succeed. I think it's important to understand that "diversity" is not the same as Affirmative Action. Affirmative Action is important and we work hard to comply within the letter and spirit of the law. Diversity extends beyond Affirmative Action in that it is not solely based on increasing the representation of various types of people in the workplace. The focus of diversity—which builds on workplace-equity initiatives—is recognizing the uniqueness of everyone, valuing the contribution that every individual can make and creating an inclusive work environment where everyone is respected and valued.

To me, it means respect for the individual. That's what I wanted and what we needed at Dial.

We faced incredible challenges from both business and workforce perspectives. We needed an integrated effort to manage the changes required and put in place a strong foundation for future success. We got to work and focused on all of the elements that drive change. And we integrated a focus on Diversity throughout all of our efforts. We needed to have *Open & Honest Communication.* We needed to define the *desired culture and working environment* as well as our business goals. We had to influence *leadership behavior and ensure accountability.*

While there was a lot of anxiety in the organization and employee morale was at an all-time low because of the Company's poor business performance and low respect for the individual, we needed to make sure we had *engaged and informed employees. Formal feedback mechanisms on behavior and development* had to be developed and implemented. We needed to put in place *recognition and rewards* that reinforced our business goals and our desired culture, and we needed to *measure our progress* on all of these fronts.

Here are some examples of what we did:

One of my first acts after taking the CEO position was to meet with our people and tell them candidly where we were headed. We promised four things: Integrity, Fairness, Candor, and Action. We said we would establish trust and maintain the highest standards of honesty and integrity with not only our investors and customers, but, most importantly, with our employees. We established regular forums where employees could ask questions and hear answers directly from management, and we created an open and available style of management.

Open and honest communication was critical as we initiated our diversity efforts. Employees needed to hear it straight from me. We also needed to hear from employees. External diversity consultants conducted individual interviews with approximately 350 employees throughout the Company. They gathered detailed information and feedback about our organization and business plans. This organizational assessment provided input for developing our strategy and implementation plan. I also started to meet with employees at all levels at informal lunches we call "Hot Dogs with Herb."

Part of our business strategy is a focus on Innovation, on being "first, fast and fresh to market" with innovative new products to meet consumers' needs. This focus on Innovation is closely linked to our Diversity efforts. Diversity in ideas, approaches and thinking styles is essential to Dial's future. Every person brings with them a unique blend of personality traits, strengths, styles and backgrounds that makes us a stronger Company. A key element of our culture change was the development of our Cultural Contract to clearly define the desired culture and working environment.

We began work on the culture immediately after I arrived at Dial. We held broad-based employee focus groups followed by an off-site senior management meeting to write the Contract. Our Cultural Contract spells out what we expect from each other—what employees expect from their colleagues and managers, and from me. It defines the way we will work together to reach business goals and it provides a strong foundation for our future success as a Company. It says a diversity of opinions is important. It says every person's ideas count. It says that we treat everyone with dignity and respect and that we are open and honest with each other. It says that we require and demonstrate ethical behavior and integrity in all our business interactions at every level in the organization. It says that we develop and leverage the abilities and perspectives of all individuals in our diverse organization.

I'm proud to say that every person at Dial has signed a Cultural Contract. They are posted in areas throughout our buildings and serve as a guidepost and reminder to help create a culture of respect, inclusion and cooperation throughout the Company.

Posters are important; however, you can put up all the posters you want but it's the actions of our leaders that will drive the kind of culture that we want and need. We had to influence *leadership behavior and ensure accountability.* Management needed to support all aspects of the Cultural Contract. Each individual had to step up to the plate and it started with me. During my first week at Dial, I spoke at our National Sales Meeting.

As I looked out over the audience, it struck me that I did not see the diversity of our customers and consumers reflected in the audience. I said so to the group, and stated my commitment to focus on having a workforce that reflected the diversity important to our success.

To ensure accountability at the right levels in the organization, we developed measures for every function and department. We measure progress and track improvement on minority and female representation, development and promotion. In addition, the bonus of each Senior Leadership Team member is based in part on the extent to which they take advantage of opportunities to support Diversity as they make hiring and promotion decisions in their organizations. To make sure that a focus on Diversity is integrated throughout the organization, I chartered and continue to lead Dial's Diversity Leadership Team.

The role of this Team is to help set diversity strategy, integrate efforts with business goals, influence policy and programs, and measure progress. Members of this Team represent a cross-functional group of senior employees who help drive the change into the organization. I am proud that Dial's leadership and focus on Diversity extends beyond the Company.

We contribute and provide ongoing support to community organizations whose efforts support and develop diverse populations. Dial also provides support to events focused on the needs of diverse communities. When I took over as CEO two years ago, there was a lot of anxiety in the organization and employee morale was at an all-time low.

We needed to make sure we had *engaged and informed employees.* From a Diversity perspective, we addressed this on several fronts. We developed a two-part formal Mentoring Program that is available to every employee. We also put efforts in place to increase awareness and respect for Diversity in our workplace. These are important values at Dial. Our goal is to go beyond the old notions of affirmative action to develop and leverage the abilities of all individuals in the organization.

To support our goal, all Dial employees are in the process of attending a workshop, *"Diversity Excellence Through Mutualism at Dial."*

This past May, we hosted a Diversity Week, a highlight of which was an all-employee Diversity Day. It was a day that one person described as *"a major step in the right direction for Dial."* People from Dial Headquarters, the Dial Center for Innovation, Dial plants and Field Sales spent the day learning about Diversity and what it means in the marketplace, what it means to Dial, and what it means to each individual.

The week made a strong statement to the workforce that Dial values diversity. A strong case was made for diversity as a sound business strategy. During Diversity Week, we held a "Diversity Showcase" where employees were invited to be part of Diversity Week. They loaned items for a museum-like display representing their own personal heritage. The result was a meaningful representation of the diverse backgrounds of Dial employees. To remind employees to value Diversity, we have posters located throughout all of our buildings at all locations. One poster, titled "Instruments," shows a series of instruments typically seen in an orchestra. Its message says that played alone, each instrument creates a unique sound. Played together, they make music!

The posters reflect on what makes each individual unique, and remind us to consider how, when we work together, when we respect and value differences, we are more effective. To make sure that diversity is integrated in all that we do, Diversity Action Teams have been formed with broad-based employee membership. These "DATS" include:

The Training Diversity Action Team, which is focused on building awareness around the concept of diversity.

The Ethnic Marketing Diversity Action Team which has identified Hispanic and Asian markets as target areas to explore and on which to concentrate.

The Recruitment and Retention Diversity Action Team is focused on three areas:

- enhancing the Diversity Recruitment Strategy developed by HR
- developing a proactive College Recruitment Plan, and
- tools and processes to develop and retain high-potential employees

The Communication and Awareness Diversity Action Team facilitates ongoing communication on Diversity progress and programs to build awareness and understanding at all levels in the Company. Dial is also committed to supporting Diversity in our supplier base. We have an active Dial Supplier Diversity Team. Its goal is to develop mutually beneficial business relationships with diverse suppliers that have a positive and lasting impact both for Dial and in the communities where we do business.

To make sure our change took root, we developed *formal feedback mechanisms* on behavior and development. We implemented the Performance & Career Development Program (PCD), which is linked to our succession-planning process. PCD was established to strengthen career development within the Company for all employees.

The four components of PCD, which occur throughout the year are: Performance Planning; ongoing Coaching and Feedback; Career Development Planning; Annual Performance Review.

In addition, we have instituted a formal leadership-development program for my Senior Leadership Team. It includes 360-degree feedback and defines each person's profile in relation to the competencies critical to our success. Behaviors supporting our Diversity strategy are integrated throughout the feedback. We need to make sure that we *measure our progress* on all of these fronts.

As I already mentioned, we track our progress on important individual department-specific Diversity measures. We also measure our progress on how we are doing against the Cultural Contract throughout the Company with an annual Employee Culture Survey. The survey questions include several that are specific to our Diversity efforts.

We've just completed this year's survey, and 75% of employees responded. While results have not been tabulated, initial indications are quite encouraging and positive.

I review and analyze the results of the survey with my Leadership Team. Each department leader is accountable to put together actionable plans to address areas of concern and opportunity.

We also have instituted an Employee Advisory Council, kind of like an internal Board of Directors, that meets with me on a quarterly basis.

- We review results of the Employee Survey;
- and discuss the action plans put in place to address areas in need of improvement.

We've just distributed a *Progress Report to Employees* that outlines where we are, how far we have come and what we have yet to do.

Earlier this year, each employee participated in what we called "The Wall of Hands." This effort emphasized our core Company initiatives. Each employee placed and signed their handprint, made in paint, on a wall in our main common area and within common areas at all Dial facilities. The wall was titled with the appropriate phrase "Our Future Is in Our Hands." It's a symbolic and meaningful way for all employees to understand that their involvement and commitment is crucial to our success. It is a vivid daily reminder that each employee has an important part to play in the Company's future.

And what have been our results since August 2000?

- We have strengthened our base business.
- Earnings per share have grown at a 35% compounded annual growth rate.
- Market share is up in all of our four core businesses.
- Gross margin is up more than 600 basis points.
- And operating margin is up over 600 basis points since August of 2000.

- We have exited underperforming businesses and firmed up our balance sheet.

We've made progress on the people side as well:

- The percentage of women in senior leadership (vice presidents and above) is over 25%.
- Since January, 41.6% of all promotions to Director level and above are women and 12.5% are minorities.
- Female Directors up 5%, female managers up 12% and minority managers up 4% over last year.
- We've seen an increase in the number of women and minorities hired.
- Year-to-date, 59% of salaried new hires across the Company were female and 23% were minorities.
- We've reduced overall turnover to 6%, its lowest level in eleven years.

We're focused on the innovation and diversity of people and ideas to drive our future growth. And I'm confident we will succeed. We have the necessary commitment, leadership and support to create the diverse workforce and the right work environment that is critical to our success. I'll end with a short video prepared last month when Dial won the Corporate Advocate Award for our support of Women and Minority Owned Businesses. In it, you'll see our Headquarters Building, some of our employees and our Wall of Hands.

As stated in our Cultural Contract, "We will develop and leverage the abilities and perspectives of all individuals in our diverse organization." And we are and will be a stronger and more successful Company because of our efforts.

QUAKER STATE 1998 ANNUAL MEETING SPEECH

HERBERT M. BAUM, Chairman and Chief Executive Officer

Good afternoon, and welcome to the annual meeting of Quaker State Corporation. I am very glad to be speaking to you at a historic turning point for our company. Through five years of dramatic change, Quaker State has emerged as a new and dynamic business. We have transformed ourselves from a loose string of unrelated companies including commodity-based motor oil into a high-performance, higher margin consumer car care company, with a stable of exciting, popular and profitable automotive brands.

Now we are about to take this *new* Quaker State to an even higher level. We have agreed to a merger with the Pennzoil Company's downstream operations, which we believe will create an industry powerhouse—the Procter & Gamble of the automotive aftermarket industry. Our new, larger and more efficient company will have premier automotive brands in a wide range of categories, covering just about every consumer need for car protection—bumper-to-bumper, inside and out.

The closing, which we hope will occur by year-end, is subject to a number of conditions, including the expiration of the Hart-Scott-Rodino Antitrust Act's waiting period, receipt of a ruling from the Internal Revenue Service to the effect that the spin-off of Pennzoil's downstream operations will be tax-free and the approval of our stockholders.

The terms of the merger, the reasons for the merger and other important information will be set forth in detail in a proxy statement that will be sent to all of Quaker State's stockholders in advance of the special meeting that will be called to vote upon approval of the merger. There will also be a prospectus registering the shares of the new company to be spun off from Pennzoil to be issued to Quaker State stockholders in the merger. Because of legal requirements for proxy statements and registered offerings, I have been advised that we must limit our comments on the proposed merger at this meeting . . . although I'll have a few words later on.

Our theme for this past year has been "putting it all together"—and that is just what we have done. We have put together a business primed for sustainable growth and increased shareowner value. From the outset, we need to keep in mind that we have built a stronger, more competitive Quaker

State. We should be proud of what we have achieved and confident in our future—whatever the final outcome of the transaction with Pennzoil. We are proceeding assuredly on the assumption that our merger will receive regulatory and shareowner approvals. Nonetheless, we must not lose sight of the viability and vigor of the New Quaker State in its own right. We have created a dynamic growth strategy. We are implementing that strategy, and we are realizing clear and significant benefits from it as we prepare our company for the future.

To appreciate where we are going, we have to first understand how we got to where we are and what it all means. I will make that the focus of my remarks today. During the past five years, we have taken Quaker State, which was a rudderless ship, on a journey to restore and enhance its value in the midst of a changing competitive environment. Our objective in the coming years must be to maintain that course of growth and profitability.

We have come a long way forward, as a number of key indicators reveal. Since I became CEO in 1993, Quaker State's revenues have more than doubled, from about a half-billion dollars to more than a billion.

Our pre-tax income from continuing operations has soared, from less than $4 million in 1993 to more than $22 million in 1997. Net income overall grew nearly 70 percent, to more than $23 million. Stockholders' equity has jumped more than 75 percent in five years. Operating margins before special charges have gone from less than 1 percent to more than 3 percent. And our market share for motor oil has climbed from 12.5 percent in 1993 to 14.5 percent in 1997 . . . two full points in one of the toughest market segments around. These measured achievements indicate the success of our strategy to transform Quaker State into a high-performance car care company.

In 1997, we reached our goal of becoming a total car care company with a sharpened focus and a clear sense of mission. We have moved from an unfocused mini-conglomerate to a very focused leading provider of branded consumer car care products and services. We have become more customer-centered than ever, and reestablished Quaker State as a premier innovator and marketer with the introduction of new and exciting products.

This has been a long and difficult process. Our share price over the years has not reflected the true performance of the company because we have had to pay for the sins of the past while paving the way for the future. Special charges in each year since 1993 have overshadowed excellent growth in all of our businesses. For instance in 1993, we had to pay $6 million to settle a Heritage Insurance lawsuit stemming from the termination of an agent that took place approximately ten years ago. But this management paid for it. Our too-long-delayed move from Oil City to Dallas in 1995 cost nearly $14 million. That year, we also had to pay nearly $2.7 million to settle a class-action lawsuit alleging price fixing going back to 1981. That hurt the stock price. The write-down to a realizable sale value of our non-strategic Newell, West Virginia, refinery in 1996 cost us $12 million in earnings and forced us to contend with substantial charges for environmental clean-up of problems accumulated over the years. But this management paid for it.

In addition, last year we incurred a charge of $3 million due to losses under a petroleum-based wax contract, first negotiated in 1990 (before this management was in place). All of these costs stemmed from events of long ago that preceded "the new Quaker State" . . . and had an impact on our earnings which has served to suppress our stock price over the past several years. But all were necessary for the rebuilding of Quaker State into a powerful and profitable company. Despite the changes, we continued to grow our revenues, our income from continuing operations, our net income, our operating margins and our market share. We endured short-term pain for long-term gain . . . getting this company prepared for what it is today. And now, Quaker State has prepared for an even bigger future . . . as part of a combined company with Pennzoil Products. Consolidation within the car care industry is a fact of life—and we and Pennzoil have led the way.

A key to past growth has been the refocusing of our business through acquisitions and divestitures. Our strategy has been to divest lower-margin commodity businesses and non-core manufacturing operations. This gave us the wherewithal to expand our portfolio with more profitable consumer automotive brands and services. Last year saw major milestones in both these processes. In July, we exited the pipeline and refining businesses with the sale of our Newell, West Virginia, refinery and associated assets for approximately $40 million. In November, we completed the sale of Truck-Lite, our safety lighting subsidiary, to Penske Capital Partners for $82 million.

Meanwhile, we expanded our thoroughbred stable of consumer brands. In August 1997, we acquired Axius Holdings, L.P., for approximately $51 million. Axius is a leading marketer of automotive sun protection products under the Auto-Shade brand. They also make a full range of quality automotive accessories such as organizers and steering wheel covers. You have seen a sampling of their products in the anteroom outside this meeting.

Then in November we purchased Rain-X, the number-one brand of automotive glass water repellant treatments. Rain-X is a well recognized brand which we believe has outstanding growth potential in North America and abroad. These additions complement the other powerful consumer automotive brands we have acquired during the past two years: Slick 50 engine and fuel treatments, the Blue Coral line of appearance products, and Medo air fresheners. We now offer enhancements for nearly every aspect of a car's performance and appearance.

Having refocused our business and resolved the issues of the past, we finally have a clean slate. We began putting it all together with a comprehensive restructuring program, which we announced in December of 1997. This restructuring plan was designed to organize our businesses in a more coordinated and streamlined fashion in order to:

- fully leverage the synergies from our recent acquisitions;
- significantly reduce costs at every level; and
- employ new information systems technology to maximize efficiency and ensure unparalleled customer service.

Our customers demand customized and efficient service to pare inventories, reduce costs, streamline operations and maintain their competitive edge. By offering best-in-class customer service—at lower cost—we help our customers achieve their goals and ensure ourselves a lasting advantage as a preferred provider. This customer focus will remain a key element of our ongoing growth strategy.

Our company's financial performance in 1997 reflected our new focus and product range. Net income for the year increased 68 percent, to more than $23 million, or $0.66 per share, compared with 1996 net income of nearly $14 million, or $0.40 per share. Revenues (which include no price increases) jumped 7.2 percent over the prior year, to about $1.2 billion. Who says the automotive aftermarket is a slow growth business?

Our 1997 net income included after-tax charges of $29.5 million, or $0.84 per share, to cover restructuring, systems improvements and other non-recurring special items, such as those related to the environmental costs associated with the sale of our refinery business. These charges offset a 1997 gain of approximately $25.9 million, or $0.74 per share, primarily from the sale of our Truck-Lite subsidiary. The special charges were absolutely necessary to get our lubricants businesses to a higher level of profitability and optimize the strong earnings potential of our consumer products businesses.

Income from continuing operations, before special charges, increased 17 percent, to $22.2 million, or $0.63 per share, versus almost $18.9 million, or $0.55 per share, for 1996. This was largely due to the inclusion of full-year results for Blue Coral and Medo. Stockholders' equity for 1997 was $331.9 million, or $9.15 per share, compared to $298.6 million, or $8.60 per share, in 1996.

Despite a declining motor oil market, Quaker State branded lubricants volume grew 3 percent, and the market share for Quaker State's branded motor oil moved up to 14.5 percent in the U.S. Even with these gains, revenues and operating profit fell for our core lubricants businesses, reflecting primarily the sale of our refinery business, poor refining margins prior to the sale, and higher marketing, distribution and operating costs. We intend to deal with these cost issues through our restructuring and supply chain initiatives in 1998 and beyond.

In 1997, the Consumer Products Group excelled as revenues for this segment doubled and operating profit tripled over the previous year—largely due to the inclusion of full-year results from Blue Coral and Medo. From zero just three years ago, our Consumer Products Group now accounts for 24 percent of our total revenues and 57 percent of our operating profit. Its performance raised our overall margins in the face of lower-margin lubricant sales.

A critical success factor for our brands is innovation. In 1997 Quaker State launched dramatically new products in nearly every market segment. In addition to their outstanding quality, these products also offer the added bonus of higher-margin returns.

Last year, we introduced three synthetic motor oils: High Performance Premium synthetic blend for high-horsepower engines; Synchron Ultra Premium full synthetic for ultimate engine protection; and 4X4 Special Synthetic Blend for hard-working engines. Each is packaged in a clear bottle to highlight the patented Micro-Q Filtration process, which we use to produce motor oils that are exceptionally pure and clean. We introduced this new line because it is what consumers told us they wanted. Our new line of motor oils has a unique shelf presence and has created meaningful excitement among retailers as well as consumers.

Innovation was the word at Blue Coral as well. Blue Coral Self Dry Car Wash and Self Clean products offer one-step convenience and quality for car and tire care. We have incorporated the superior protection of Teflon into Blue Coral's new Professional Gel Car Wash, Gel Wax and Gel Protectant products. And Slick 50 expanded its product lines with new, advanced synthetic engine treatment and auto polish products under the Synchron name.

By every measure, we built up great momentum in 1997, and we carried through on that momentum in the first quarter of 1998. Our earnings met the market's expectations of 15 cents per share before unusual items. Our branded motor oil sales increased 10 percent for the quarter, despite the softness in the overall market. We are glad to see this growth continuing through April, and we are optimistic that we can sustain strong growth in our branded motor oil business throughout the second quarter.

Operating profit for Lubricants and Lubricant Services in the first quarter was up 13 percent. Revenues for the segment, though, were lower than last year, reflecting the absence of refinery by-product sales associated with the sale of the refinery business.

As for Consumer Products, sales in the first quarter jumped nearly 22 percent with the inclusion of Axius and Rain-X. Operating profit declined slightly, due primarily to a change in our product mix, higher advertising and marketing costs and the timing of promotional activities. Importantly, the operating profit margin for our Consumer Products segment was nearly three times as large as that for Lubricants and Lubricant Services. This demonstrates the powerful impact of our portfolio restructuring, as the Consumer Products segment contributed 54 percent of our first-quarter operating earnings on 29 percent of our total sales revenues.

Our results for the past fifteen months indicate that we are turning the corner just as we said we would. This is a tribute to the dedication and hard work of Quaker State employees in every segment of our company. I am happy to see a number of my colleagues with us at today's annual meeting. On behalf of all Quaker State shareowners, I want to thank our employees—both here and around the world—for their tireless effort and support during this transition period. We appreciate your devotion to the dream of a new and better Quaker State. Your management team is doing everything possible to realize that dream and to take our brands and businesses forward into a new century of growth.

To do that, we also must realize that our rebuilding process is never-ending. We must continually improve our operations, enhance our service, cut our costs and increase our efficiency. We believe our proposed merger with Pennzoil is the natural next step in that progression. As we said when we announced the agreement, a merger of this kind will combine the best of both businesses, complement our mix of brands and services and generate major synergies and significant cost savings that we expect will have a positive impact on shareowner value.

If you look at any industry—from banking to pharmaceuticals to transportation to food—you can see that size matters. A growing number of companies are turning to consolidation as a way to expand their markets, cut their costs and maintain their global competitiveness. Growth must come from lower costs in today's low-inflation economy. As a recent article in *Money* magazine put it, "Falling inflation has made it harder for companies to generate profits by raising prices, so businesses have to remain relentless about slashing costs. A merger that consolidates operations offers great opportunities to increase efficiency and boost earnings."

The article also noted that today's "best mergers" are those that "are strategic and offer the potential for far greater long-term profits"—as opposed to a quick gain on the purchase of an undervalued company. Sometimes it takes patience, but great rewards can come to those who invest in the future.

Now, what about the Pennzoil merger? SEC rules do not permit us to discuss our agreement with Pennzoil in detail during this so-called "quiet period," but we do expect to be able to make a full presentation to shareholders and Wall Street analysts later this summer. That should help investors and analysts make a fair assessment for themselves.

As to the future, we believe Quaker State will be strong and full of growth. We have taken our brands out of the shadows. We have reinvented our business. We have refocused our efforts on high-performance, higher-margin products and services. And we have returned to the fundamentals of customer service and consumer satisfaction.

The reinvention of Quaker State will continue, in one form or another, into the next millennium. The consumer demands it. The market requires it. The company's shareholders deserve it. Throughout the past five years, we have been driven to relentless, continuous improvement in our company's performance and its value. That commitment will continue to drive us forward until we emerge as the premier automotive car care company in North America . . . and, probably, the world.

INDEX